RECENT
HUNTING TRIPS
IN
NORTH AMERICA

CW00517876

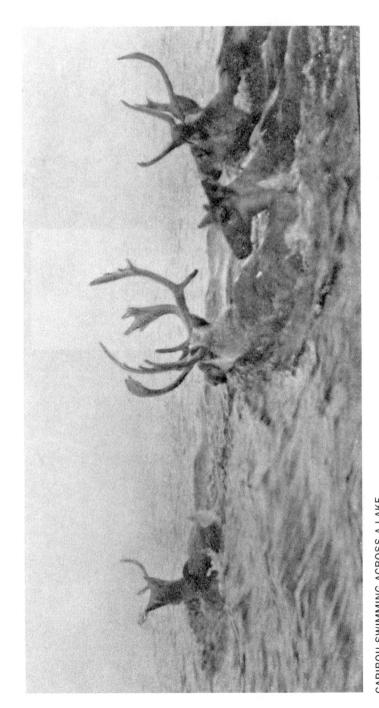

CARIBOU SWIMMING ACROSS A LAKE.
Photograph by S.H. PARSONS.

RECENT
HUNTING TRIPS
IN
NORTH AMERICA

By

F. C. SELOUS

WITH 65 ILLUSTRATIONS
FROM PHOTOGRAPHS BY THE
AUTHOR AND OTHERS

MISSOULA, MONTANA | 2021

Hunting Trips in North America

By F. C. Selous

Originally published in 1907.
Reprinted in 2021 as part of
Boone and Crockett Club's series,
B&C Classics.

Paperback ISBN: 978-1-940860-44-2
ePub ISBN: 978-1-940860-45-9
Published November 2021

Published in the United States of America
by the
Boone and Crockett Club
250 Station Drive, Missoula, Montana 59801
Phone (406) 542-1888
Fax (406) 542-0784
Toll-Free (888) 840-4868 (book orders only)
www.boone-crockett.org

MESSAGE FROM THE PUBLISHER

THE Boone and Crockett Club was founded by Theodore Roosevelt and George Bird Grinnell in 1887. Two years earlier, Grinnell, then editor of *Forest and Stream,* wrote a critical review of Roosevelt's book, *Hunting Trips of a Ranchman.* Roosevelt paid him a visit to discuss the matter. During that meeting Grinnell presented a strong case about his concerns on the future of hunting and conservation. TR was in agreement, and thus began a lifelong friendship that led to the founding of the Boone and Crockett Club, the first private hunting and conservation organization in North America. The two also went on to collaborate on numerous books about hunting, conservation, exploration, and adventure. Since its early days, B&C has had a strong tie with publishing and furthering hunting and conservation.

In 2012, we launched our B&C Classics series of hunting and adventure books, including works from TR and Grinnell, as well as William T. Hornaday, Charles Sheldon, Frederick C. Selous and other adventurers from the late 1800s through the early 1900s. Each title in the B&C Classics series is selected by a committee of vintage hunting literature experts and is authored by a Boone and Crockett Club member.

Unlike other reprints of these hunting and adventure books, the B&C Classics series has been meticulously converted resulting in high-quality, digitally remastered eBooks and paperback editions. Many are complete with vintage photos and drawings not found in other editions. This attention to detail helps transport readers back to a time when hunting trips didn't happen over a weekend, but were adventures that spanned weeks, months, or even years.

We hope you enjoy the books we've selected for this series. They will give you a strong sense of our hunting heritage and provide hours of entertainment for anyone who loves adventure and the outdoors.

JULIE L. TRIPP
B&C Director of Publications
MISSOULA, MONTANA

TO ALL MY MANY KIND
FRIENDS IN CANADA,
NEWFOUNDLAND
AND THE UNITED
STATES OF AMERICA,
THIS BOOK IS CORDIALLY
DEDICATED.

ON LAKE BOIS FRANC.
George Crawford in a birch-bark canoe.

PREFACE

ALL the best years of my life, from youth till middle age, were spent as a hunter of African game. During that time the love of the free wandering life in countries still well stocked with the richest and most varied fauna to be found on the face of the earth, grew with the years, till it seemed to me that I could never be content to live any other life than that of a nomadic hunter.

But as time went on the game that was of value became ever scarcer and scarcer, civilization gradually spread over the old hunting grounds, and the old hunters either died or had to turn their energies in other directions.

It is now a good many years since I ceased to make my living by my rifle, but in view of the length of time during which I did so, and the eventful character of the life I then led, it is not, perhaps, remarkable that my thoughts still often wander back to a past of stirring and glorious memories. Nor is it surprising that I sometimes grow restless and dissatisfied with life in this highly civilized country, and long with an irresistible longing to taste the joys of a hunter's life once more.

Those to whose lot it will fall to criticise this book, will possibly find it more surprising that I should have had the hardihood, after having already written so much on the subject of sport and travel, to publish the record of the few unimportant hunting trips which have been the outcome of my restlessness during the last few years.

I can only hope that in these transcripts from my diaries, written nightly over the camp fire, when the events described were fresh in my memory, they will find here and there matter of sufficient interest to incline them to extend to me once more the same kindly consideration they have always given me in the past.

With the ever-growing brotherhood of young and vigorous big game hunters, I cherish the hope that this plain tale of the latest wanderings of an elder brother of the craft may find some favour. May it not only afford interest and information, but act as an incentive to the undertaking of hunting trips to one or other of those vast and still unexplored hunting fields of North-western Canada, which are still almost virgin ground to the British sportsman.

American Alaska, in the central portions of which all the species of great game inhabiting the far north-west of the American Continent, are still extraordinarily plentiful, is at present closed to the sportsman. Closed, too, by laws which do not seem to have been inspired by any great measure of common sense. For although the few wandering sportsmen, who under kinder legislation might visit the country, and spend a good deal of money in it, for the sake of a few good heads of moose, caribou and wild sheep, are inexorably barred out, the game is by no means being preserved.

The Indians, now no longer armed only with the archaic weapons of their forefathers, but with Winchester rifles of the latest pattern, kill what they will, without any restraint, and find a market at the mining camps for all the meat they can bring in; whilst white meat hunters are equally destructive. Prospectors and trappers, though they do not often destroy game unnecessarily, are each and every one of them more harmful to the wild fauna of the country than the average sportsman, because they kill whatever comes first to hand, whilst the latter seldom shoots anything but old males, the elimination of which does not reduce the power of increase of a species.

One often reads some very caustic criticisms concerning the selfishness, and thoughtless savagery of the head-hunting sportsman, and I admit that it is quite arguable that the Indian hunter or white prospector or trapper who shoots a lot of female moose, caribou or wild sheep, in order to provide himself with a supply of meat for the winter, has a better justification for what he does. He has the justification of necessity, which the sportsman has not. Still it is the men who live in the country, and who of necessity are constantly killing the game, without regard to age or sex, who will gradually bring about its extinction; not the casual sportsman looking for a few good heads of old males.

Loving as I do—with the passionate love of one, all the best years of whose life were spent in the wilderness—the sight of wild animals in their natural surroundings, I look upon the gradual extermination of game throughout the world by the encroachments of civilization upon their haunts, with the utmost regret. Consequently I am of the opinion that Mr. E. N. Buxton and his colleagues deserve the warmest thanks of all lovers of wild life, for the strenuous efforts they have made and are making to preserve from destruction the wild fauna of the Empire.

However, there are yet vast areas of British Africa and the far north and west of British North America, where big game is plentiful, and where Europeans will probably never settle down. In such wild and inhospitable regions I hope and believe that if the game is not exterminated by natives armed with modern weapons, well stocked hunting grounds will be available for enterprising and energetic British sportsmen of moderate desires for a long time yet to come.

In the following chapters will be found a description of my first moose hunt in Central Canada, together with accounts of caribou hunting off the beaten tracks in Newfoundland, and the pursuit of moose, wild sheep, and caribou in the almost virgin hunting grounds of the Yukon Territory of Northwestern Canada. Where I hunted moose near Lake Kippewa seven years ago, is now I believe the centre of a great mining district; but in Newfoundland and the Yukon Territory the conditions will be found much as I have described them, probably for a long time yet to come.

When I first visited Newfoundland in 1900, I found that caribou hunting was almost entirely confined to shooting these animals from ambushes, as they passed southwards across the railway on migration to their winter feeding grounds. This form of sport had no attraction whatever for me, and I, therefore, left the railway and made a little trip southwards to St. John's Pond.

On this trip I was not very successful in finding caribou, but I convinced myself that considerable numbers of these animals never went north across the railway line in the spring, but remained the whole year round in the centre of the island. I saw, too, that the only way to get to this country would be by canoe up one of the shallow rocky rivers which take their rise in the interior of the island.

At that time there was not a canoe to be had anywhere in Newfoundland—only heavy boats with which it was impossible to get far up any of the smaller rivers. So in 1901 I imported a sixteen-foot bass wood canoe from Canada, and a canvas folding canoe from America, and with their help reached St. John's Pond without much difficulty and carried out a successful hunting trip in the country to the south-west of the lake. No British or native white sportsman had I believe ever shot there before, and, indeed, much of the country I traversed was, I believe, wholly unexplored.

As far as I know it was this successful hunting trip of mine to the interior of Newfoundland by means of canoes in 1901, which first turned the eyes of the more energetic of those sportsmen who have visited the island in recent years, to the possibilities of the sport to be obtained in the unknown interior of the country. My friend, Mr. J. G. Millais, has gone far beyond me, on the path I think I first pointed out, and during the last few years has explored much of the interior of the island, discovered much well-stocked deer ground, and brought home the most magnificent collection of caribou heads ever shot by one man. That ardent and energetic young big game hunter, Mr. H. Hesketh Prichard, too, as well as several other well-known sportsmen, have also recently made successful journeys to the interior of Newfoundland in search of caribou.

In 1905 I paid my third and last visit to Newfoundland, and with the help of a canoe and two good men, penetrated from Red Indian Lake to King George the Fourth's Lake, which I believe had only twice previously been visited by white men; the last visit having been that of Mr. Howley, the veteran surveyor of Newfoundland, thirty years previously.

In 1904 and again in 1906, I visited the Yukon Territory of North-western Canada, and made two very successful hunting trips up the Macmillan River. Up to 1902 this fine stream was absolutely unknown except to a few trappers. During that year, however, a surveying party under the leadership of Mr. R. G. MacConnell was sent from Dawson by the Canadian Geological Survey to explore its course.

The country, however, lying between the north and the south forks of the Macmillan and north and south of both those streams still remained entirely unknown and unexplored, so that when in 1904 Mr. Sheldon and I hunted over the mountain ranges lying just south of the north fork, we were in a country where in all probability the foot of a white man had never trodden before.

We had with us but one man a piece, and as the country in which we found ourselves was absolutely uninhabited, Indian guides or packers were unobtainable, and we had therefore to carry all our camp-gear, blankets and provisions up into the mountains on our own backs, and thus hunted under great difficulties; but still with fair success, all things considered.

We could not move about much, and so did not cover much ground, and thus failed to find the wild sheep rams of which my friend was particularly anxious to secure specimens. We saw a good many ewes and lambs, however, so that the rams must also have been in the district, and we should no doubt have found them had we had any means of transport save our own backs.

During this trip I had the good fortune to shoot a magnificent specimen of a moose, carrying a head which rivals in size and weight all but the finest heads of the giant species of moose (*Alces gigas*) found in the Kenai Peninsula of Alaska.

In 1906 I reached the upper waters of the south fork of the Macmillan River after twenty-two days' hard work against a very strong stream after leaving the Yukon River.

During this trip I secured several fine specimens of Osborn's caribou, the largest and handsomest species of caribou that exists, and was also fortunate enough to shoot another moose with a very fine head. I also shot a fine specimen of a black wolf.

The entire skin of my finest caribou I preserved and presented to the trustees of the Natural History Museum at South Kensington, together with the complete skin of a Newfoundland caribou which I shot and preserved in 1905. These two specimens, splendidly mounted by Rowland Ward, of Piccadilly, may now be seen in the Mammalian Gallery of the Museum, and form, I think, an interesting addition to our unrivalled zoological collection.

Many of the photographs which illustrate this book were taken by myself, but my best thanks are due to Mr. S. H. Parsons, of St. John's, Newfoundland, who has given me permission to make use of some very excellent pictures of caribou swimming, and other subjects, as also to my American and Canadian friends, Messrs. Sheldon, Osgood, Rungius and Cameron, who were hunting on the Macmillan River in 1904, all of whom have placed at my disposal complete sets of the photographs they took during that year.

F. C. Selous.

Worplesdon, Surrey,
April 26th, 1907.

CONTENTS

CHAPTER I.

A MOOSE HUNT IN THE FORESTS
OF CENTRAL CANADA.

CHAPTER II.

AFTER WOODLAND CARIBOU
IN NEWFOUNDLAND.

CHAPTER III.

BEYOND ST. JOHN's LAKE. A WELL STOCKED HUNTING GROUND.

CHAPTER IV.

HUNTING ON THE NORTH FORK OF THE MACMILLAN RIVER, YUKON TERRITORY.

CHAPTER V.

HOW WE FARED IN THE YUKON MOUNTAINS.

CHAPTER VI.

THE LUCK OF A HUNTER. A BIG MOOSE.

CHAPTER VII.
A JOURNEY TO KING GEORGE's LAKE, NEWFOUNDLAND.

CHAPTER VIII.
HUNTING ON THE SOUTH FORK OF THE MACMILLAN RIVER.

CHAPTER IX.

SPORT WITH BIG GAME IN THE MOUNTAINS OF THE MACMILLAN.

CHAPTER X.

HINTS ON EQUIPMENT.

LIST OF ILLUSTRATIONS.

RECENT
HUNTING TRIPS
IN
NORTH AMERICA

HEAD OF MOOSE SHOT OCT. 1, 1900.
Note the shape of the nose and
the smallness of the eye.

CHAPTER I.

A MOOSE HUNT IN THE FORESTS OF CENTRAL CANADA.

IT HAD ALWAYS been one of my ambitions to visit some district of the great North American Continent where moose were still to be found, and to hunt this giant deer in its native haunts.

For many a long year, however, Fate decreed that my life was to be passed in a part of the world far removed from the great northland, and gradually the hope of ever seeing one of these quaint ungainly old-time looking beasts grew somewhat faint, though it never entirely left me.

However "tout vient à qui sait attendre," or rather, if I may paraphrase that familiar French saying, "He who really wants a thing will sooner or later get an opportunity to go after it," and so in the autumn of 1900 the chance came to me to make a hunt after moose.

Having made some preliminary arrangements by letter, I arrived at Mattawa, in the Province of Ontario, Canada, on the evening of September 24th, bringing with me a single-shot .303 bore rifle, a few cartridges loaded with Dum-dum bullets, and a kit bag containing blankets and spare clothing. At Mattawa I purchased a supply of provisions at the Hudson's

Bay Company's store and hired for the trip a few cooking utensils, two small tents and two birch-bark canoes.

With the kind assistance of Mr. Colin G. Rankin and Mr. E. O. Taylor, the superintendent and manager of the Company's business at Mattawa, I got everything packed the day after my arrival, and on the morning of September 27th took the train to Lake Kippewa, accompanied by a half-breed guide named George Crawford, and his boy Joe. I found George Crawford a keen and experienced hunter, and a most excellent fellow in every way, and his nephew Joe, who was almost a full-blooded Indian, a very good tempered willing servant, and a wonderful packer, for, although only fourteen years of age, he thought nothing of carrying a load of eighty pounds.

I must confess that during my two days' stay at Mattawa I was somewhat taken aback by the number of hunting parties constantly arriving there from various parts of the United States and Canada, all intent on securing that much-coveted trophy, a fine moose head. However, I reflected that the country in which all these eager sportsmen, I among them, were about to hunt, was very vast, and covered entirely, except for its rivers and lakes, with forests of a density which must be seen to be understood, and concluded that there were probably enough bull moose in these primeval solitudes for all of us, if we could only find them.

A three hours' journey by rail brought us to the southwestern shore of Lake Kippewa, where we embarked on a fine steamer—the "Hurdman"—which is employed in carrying stores to the various lumber camps on the lake shore, and which bore us forthwith across Lake Kippewa, and then through Hunter's Lake to an old abandoned landing stage, distant about a mile and a half from Lake Bois Franc.

The passage through the various sheets of water known collectively as Lake Kippewa, all of which are studded with innumerable islands, amongst which the steamer threads its way often through very narrow channels, would have been a most interesting experience had the weather been bright and fine, with the sun shining on the forests with which every island on the lake, and every portion of the mainland that was visible, is covered. Forests in which the dark-foliaged spruce and balsam are intermingled with the maple, and birch, whose leaves were now all glorious with the rich and varied tints which mark the advent of the Indian summer. But the sky was dull and threatening, and entirely obscured with rain-charged clouds, which hung low over land and water, whilst a cold wind blew from the north which was far from comfortable.

We pitched our tents that night near the old landing stage, and the next morning, which was bright and fine after the sun had dispersed the mists, carried all our belongings over a rough trail through the forest to the nearest point on Lake Bois Franc. It took us three journeys to get everything across. On one of these, George Crawford excited my admiration by carrying a bag of flour (100 lbs.) on his back, and the heaviest of the canoes, weighing probably another eighty pounds, balanced on his head. With this load he walked the mile and a half of the portage without stopping to rest.

I found the Indian way of carrying a pack, the weight of which, though it rests on one's back, is supported to a considerable extent by a broad leather strap passed across the forehead, a most excellent one, and the easiest method of carrying a heavy load, though liable at first, and especially when walking on uneven ground, to strain severely the muscles of the neck.

After having repacked the canoes, we embarked on Lake Bois Franc, and paddled about three miles to an old lumber camp, where we established our headquarters. In the afternoon we paddled to the other end of the lake, some distance up a beautiful little creek, on the sandy bottom of which we saw a few moose tracks not very old. We passed several great northern divers on the lake, and noticed a good many grebes, somewhat larger than our English dabchick. We remained in the creek until the evening, and then George gave some calls on his birch bark trumpet, in imitation of the bellow of the moose cow. These calls, though repeated at intervals until it became dark, were, however, unheard, or at any rate met with no response from a bull.

During the night it again came on to rain, and continued to do so until after noon the next day. As soon as it cleared up a bit, George and I paddled across the lake, and threaded our way through the dripping woods to a small lagoon about two miles distant. Here we saw a good many moose tracks, some of them evidently those of large bulls, so we determined to fetch one of our small tents as quickly as possible, and then hunt the surrounding country.

Accordingly, on September 30th, we carried a tent and the smaller of our two canoes, together with blankets and a few days' provisions, to this promising-looking hunting ground. In the evening, George again called for moose until long after dark, but there was no reply, and but for the occasional hooting of an owl, the great forests by which we were surrounded were absolutely voiceless.

The next day was the first of October, the opening day of the hunting season in the county of Pontiac, Province of Quebec, and in the early morning George and I set out to look for moose, following an old lumberer's trail which after a mile or so brought us to a small swampy lagoon. Here George gave a call on his birch bark trumpet, and shortly afterwards, an animal which I of course thought was a bull moose, bellowed loudly not far away in the forest behind us. George, however, pronounced it to be a cow and not a bull moose.

Thinking that there might be a bull in company with her,

we at once commenced to make our way in her direction, skirting along the lagoon just within the shelter of the forest, which grew to the very edge of the water. Before we had gone very far George who was in front, stopped suddenly, saying that he had heard something in the forest behind us like the noise of a bull's horns brushing through the spruce trees. This sound had been quite inaudible to me, as African malarial fever, or the large quantity of quinine I have taken to counteract that malady, has somewhat dulled my sense of hearing; but I soon heard a distinct rustling in the bushes, and then the sound as of some large animal walking in shallow water.

"It's a bull," whispered George; "he's coming towards us along the edge of the lake."

There was apparently no wind at all, but we were afraid that the keen-scented animal might smell our tracks, so we started to meet it, threading our way cautiously but quickly through the forest.

As we advanced the noise made by so large an animal walking in the water became more and more distinct, so I presently stepped out beyond the edge of the timber along the trunk of a fallen tree, to see if I could get a view of it. I at once caught sight of a bull moose—the first I had ever seen—coming slowly towards me, and walking knee-deep in the water of the lake just outside the forest. It looked immense, and its horns showed up well, and appeared much larger than they really proved to be when actually measured. When I first saw it this bull moose was not more than two hundred yards away, but as it seemed to be coming much nearer along the edge of the lagoon, I thought it better not to fire at once. However, after it had come a little nearer in full view, it suddenly left the water, and turned into the forest, after first passing through some bushes growing in the lake, above which only its head and horns were visible.

We now again advanced cautiously through the forest to intercept our quarry, and heard it give two or three low grunts. Then its dark form came dimly into sight amongst the trees which grew very close together. It was not more than fifty yards off, but the stems of the trees hid it to such an extent, that, moving as it was, I should probably have missed it and hit a tree had I fired hurriedly.

As George and I had halted suddenly on the instant when the moose first became visible to us, we were not hidden from it behind the stems of trees, but we stood perfectly still, and the doomed animal never turned its head towards us nor seemed in the least suspicious of danger, but came steadily forward. It had none of that appearance of alertness or timidity usually noticeable in wild animals in countries where they are much hunted by man or constantly preyed upon by carnivorous beasts.

The bull had now changed its course, and was advancing in a line that, had it kept, would have brought it past us almost broadside on at a distance of not more than thirty yards. I was afraid, however, to wait any longer, lest an eddy of wind should betray our proximity, and as soon as I could get a clear view of the front part of its body through the trees I fired. Just at that moment it was in a dip of the ground, so that its legs and part of its body were hidden from view, and my bullet struck it rather high behind the shoulder, but this shot would certainly have proved fatal, as it pierced both lungs below the backbone. Immediately I had fired, I ran in, pushing another cartridge into the breach of my single-shot rifle as I did so.

The ground here rose rather steeply from the lake, and the wounded moose went straight up hill, but after going some twenty yards, stopped and, turning broadside, looked back, giving me a splendid second chance, of which I was not slow to take advantage. At this second shot, which pierced its heart, the giant deer gave a spasmodic plunge forward, and then rolled over dead.

I was mightily pleased to have at last shot a fairly good specimen of a bull moose. George pronounced it to be five years old. Its horns had a spread of forty-nine inches, and carried eighteen points, and it stood six feet one inch in perpendicular height at the withers. After taking the whole of its inside out, I skinned and quartered the carcase, and then weighed the sections with my small Austrian scale. The result was as follows:

Head with skin of neck attached	48	kilos
Rest of hide	30	"
One forequarter with greater part of neck	100	"
The other forequarter	90	"
One hindquarter	66	"
The other hindquarter	60	"
Total	**394 kilos**	

Taking the kilo at two pounds three ounces this would be equal to eight hundred and sixty-two pounds clean, which is the weight that George pronounced to be that of a fair-sized moose bull of about five years old. It was, however, in very low condition and would certainly have weighed over nine hundred pounds clean, had it been shot a month earlier, and as the paunch, intestines, liver, heart and lungs weigh about one-fourth of the total weight of an animal, its live weight at that time would have been at least one thousand two hundred pounds. An exceptionally large and fat bull moose would of course weigh a good deal more.

We soon had some meat frying in the pan, and though it was naturally neither tender nor juicy, I was glad to eat any kind of meat after having tasted nothing but bacon since leaving Mattawa.

As it was still early in the morning when the moose was shot, we were able to get back to our main camp on Lake Bois

GEORGE CRAWFORD AND THE HEAD
OF MOOSE SHOT OCT. 9, 1900.

Franc with the head and a load of meat the same evening. It took me almost the whole of the following day to skin and clean my first moose head, but in the evening George paddled me across the lake into a very nice looking creek, where he called for moose but failed to get an answer.

Whilst paddling up the creek we caught sight of a white-tailed deer standing amongst some reeds. At our approach it gave one bound and disappeared in the forest which here grew close down to the water's edge. As it jumped it threw up its broad fluffy tail, exposing the snow-white hair of the under-surface, and looking for all the world like an African reedbuck.

On October 3rd we returned to the little lake where I had shot the moose two days previously. On our way there I heard a ruffed grouse drumming, and creeping close up to it, watched it displaying itself on a fallen tree. Ultimately I cut its head off with a .303 bullet, as I thought it would make a welcome addition to my larder. It was a very handsome cock bird with a fine ruff of black feathers round the neck.

I thought it very curious that a ruffed grouse should be drumming at this time of the year, as I had imagined that, as in the case of European game birds, such manifestations were only indulged in during the breeding season, but George told me that ruffed grouse may often be heard drumming in the autumn during fine weather. In the evening we again called for moose, but got no answer and saw nothing. During the night it rained a little, and the weather became quite warm and muggy.

For another week we hunted daily and travelled many a weary mile through the sombre forests to the south of Lake Bois Franc. We happened on many beautiful little lakes and swampy lagoons, in one of which was a small beaver house evidently inhabited, as it had been recently built. Although during this time we came across three moose cows with calves and a young bull with a small head, no broad-antlered monarch of the northern forests ever crossed our path until on the morning of October 9th.

Early that day we came on the track of a big moose bull soon after leaving camp and followed it for six hours. Then we gave up the pursuit, as judging from certain signs, George declared the great deer to be so far in front of us that there was no chance of overtaking it. Taking a bee line through the forest my trusty guide brought me back to our camp at one end of a beautiful little lake late in the afternoon. It was a most lovely evening so perfectly still that there was not a ripple on the surface of the water, and when we had had something to eat, and the sun had just set, George proposed that we should paddle up to the head of the lake and try a call.

We were nearing the end of the lake, and George had laid down his paddle, and was about to raise his birch bark trumpet to his lips, when we heard a low grunt in the forest behind us. "That's a bull," whispered George; "he's coming down to the lake." We turned the canoe round as quickly as possible, and almost immediately heard a slight rustling amongst the spruce trees, and then saw a cow moose preceded by a calf, walk out into the lake until they stood knee-deep in the water.

I felt terribly disappointed, but George again whispered," It was a bull that grunted, look out, he'll be close behind the cow," and almost as he spoke, a great bull moose, the broad palms of whose antlers I at once noted, came into view.

He was but an average specimen of his race, but standing well out in the lake with head turned towards the gorgeous glow in the western sky, and with the dark spruce wood behind him, he looked grand beyond the power of words to describe. He appeared so manifestly a survival from very ancient times, that I could not help experiencing a curious feeling that the picture before me was unreal, a memory perhaps of something that I had seen ages ago, possibly in a former incarnation. But

George's eager whisper, "I'll paddle you close up, don't move," and the feel of my rifle, rudely disturbed my dream, and brought me back to the nineteenth century.

George now commenced to propel the canoe towards the family of moose, with absolute noiselessness, and although we were in full view of them it was only the calf that seemed to notice us at all, but though it looked several times intently in our direction it did not appear to suspect danger. The cow was moving slowly through the shallow water with her nose down, apparently drinking, and the bull kept pace with her a little nearer the shore, his body being almost entirely hidden by hers.

I was within seventy yards of them when the cow at last moved forwards, and left the mighty bull standing in full view. He was then almost facing the canoe with his head down on the water, either drinking or more probably eating some part of the water lilies, which were growing just where he was standing. It would have been madness to have fired at him as he stood in this position, as the bullet would in all probability have broken up in the thick skin and great muscles at the back of the neck.

So I waited, and soon he raised his head and turned a little towards the cow, and then I fired as well as I could-it was fast getting dusk-for the point of his shoulder, and saw immediately that I had hit him about right, as he flinched when the bullet struck him, and as he tried to turn I saw that his left foreleg hung useless from the shoulder. I believe this bullet would have killed him, but I fired three more into him as he turned round and stumbled towards the shore of the lake. He just managed to reach dry ground and fell dead close to the water's edge.

All this time the cow and calf had been standing quite still, looking curiously towards the canoe, and after the bull had fallen they still remained standing. Then the calf walked

THE CANOE LAUNCHED ON LAKE KIPPEWA.

very slowly and sedately to the shore, and was soon followed by the cow. On reaching the edge of the forest they halted, and, although we were now within twenty yards of them, the cow came back to the lake-side alone, and with nose outstretched, stepped up to where her lord lay dead, and stood looking at him for some time, evidently quite at a loss to understand what on earth had happened to him. She then walked slowly back to her calf, and as we stepped ashore to inspect our prize, we could still see the whitish legs of the two animals as they stood amongst the trees quite close to us. After that I paid no further attention to them.

The dead bull was a fine animal. I measured his standing height between two poles held perpendicular to one another—the one at his wither, the other at the heel of his forefoot—and I made his standing height six feet two inches to the top of his shoulders, on which grew long coarse hair quite four inches in length. George pronounced this moose to be an old bull past his prime, but his horns were quite worth having as they measured just fifty inches in greatest spread and were well palmated with eighteen points. He had evidently been fighting desperately quite lately for the possession of the cow he had attached himself to, as his head and neck had been much bruised, no doubt by blows from the horns of a rival.

I spent the following day in cleaning and preserving the headskin of my second moose, and, as my license only entitled me to shoot two of these animals—only one may now be shot—I started on October 11th for a place called Snake Lake, not far from Mattawa, where George thought I might get a white-tailed deer.

After several days still hunting, during which I saw several does and fawns, but never a buck, I at last got a shot at and killed a four-year old stag with a pretty, though not, of course, a very large, pair of horns.

On the following day, October 20th, the weather was very fine without a breath of wind, and George declared that it was useless going after deer as one's footsteps on the dead leaves which now lay six inches deep on the ground all over the hard-wood forests, would be sure to attract their attention and drive them off long before it would be possible to see and get a shot at one. As it seemed probable that this weather might last for several days, and I was anxious to get to Newfoundland before the end of the month, I resolved to bring my first hunt in the forests of Canada to an end and get back to Montreal as quickly as possible.

CHAPTER II.

AFTER WOODLAND CARIBOU IN NEWFOUNDLAND.

I LANDED IN Newfoundland early on the morning of October 26th, 1900, and started at once for Howley Station, where a telegram had informed me I would find my guide and camp equipment awaiting me. The journey by rail from Portaux-Basques to Howley occupied nine hours, but the time passed quickly, as the country we travelled through was always wild and interesting. Much of the ground was covered with dense forests of spruce and juniper, but the individual trees in these wooded tracts looked very small and slight in comparison with the giant timber, amongst whose tall and massive stems I had lately been hunting moose in Canada.

I must confess that all I heard and saw concerning caribou shooting on the evening of my arrival at Howley, impressed me most unfavourably, and all I subsequently saw of shooting these animals from ambushes during their annual migration across the railway line, confirmed my low estimation of the attractions of this form of game killing.

As I stepped from the train I saw that there were several carcases of freshly-killed caribou lying on the platform of the

FINE CARIBOU HEAD SHOT NEAR
MY CAMP, OCT., 1900.

little railway station. These were all does and fawns, which I was subsequently informed had been killed that day whilst crossing the line quite close to the station. In addition to these entire carcases there were several heads, skins, and haunches of stags, but not a good or even moderate pair of horns amongst them. Seeing me examining these trophies of the chase, my guide, who had introduced himself to me as soon as I stepped from the train, remarked jovially: "Ah! You've come to the slaughter-house now. What a pity you weren't here yesterday, the deer were crossing the line all day, and everyone got lots of shots; it was just as if a battle was going on."

In the evening I took a walk along the railway line with my guide, and learned from him all I could about caribou and the way in which they were usually shot at this season of the year.

Great numbers of caribou, I was informed—but by no means all, as I subsequently discovered—spend the summer months in the northern part of Newfoundland and winter in the south of the island. There are thus two annual migrations: in the early spring from the south to the north, and in the autumn—during September and October—from north to south; and as the railway traverses the whole island from east to west every caribou which migrates is bound to cross the line twice a year.

On migration, certain tracts of country are annually traversed, through which well-defined paths are made. These deer paths are known in Newfoundland as "leads," and during the autumn migration the usual method of securing caribou was (at the time of which I am writing) by watching a " lead " and shooting the animals from an ambush as they passed. In some cases the watcher was able to command a view of several "leads," and from time to time a rapid change of position would be necessary to cut off deer coming along a trail out of

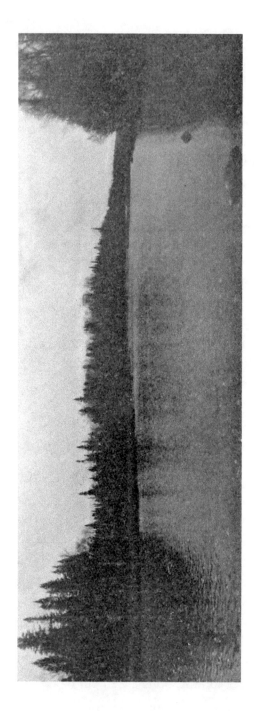

A "POND" IN THE INTERIOR
OF NEWFOUNDLAND

shot of the central ambuscade. The common practice, however, was to sit and watch all day long, and day after day, from one spot, and during this time to do no walking at all except to and from the camp on the railway line.

In watching for caribou the direction of the wind must, of course, be studied, as the sense of smell is very highly developed in these. animals, and they will at once take alarm on scenting a human being; but when on migration they travel straight ahead, and at such a time often come right down the wind, and must then trust to their eyes alone to give them notice of dangers ahead. Their eyesight is not nearly so quick as that of most wild animals, and unless they had just been shot at they always appeared to me to be absolutely unconscious that they were running any risk of encountering a lurking enemy on their line of march.

Possibly this want of alertness—so very different to the constant watchfulness displayed by African antelopes, for instance—may be due to the fact that in Newfoundland there are practically no carnivorous animals which habitually prey on the caribou. There are a few wolves, it is true, but these fierce and formidable creatures appear to be extremely scarce and, singularly enough, do not increase in numbers.

Lynxes, although now numerous in Newfoundland, have only recently established themselves on the island, and are said to be the descendants of a few enterprising individuals which, during a severe winter, crossed the Straits of Belle Isle on the ice from the neighbouring coast of Labrador. These lynxes, however, although they may occasionally catch and kill a caribou fawn, are believed to live almost entirely on hares and willow grouse. The American black bear is also found in Newfoundland, but lives principally on berries, and, although he will eat the meat of a deer which he may find lying dead, is said never to kill one of these animals himself.

Thus the caribou of Newfoundland has but one enemy—man; and even by man he is not constantly persecuted. In the year 1900 some six thousand caribou are believed to have been shot in the whole island—some seven hundred by American, British and Newfoundland sportsmen during the autumn migration, and the remainder by meat hunters during the winter, at which season the deer collect in large herds, and often approach the fishing villages on the south coast of the island. Nevertheless, the great bulk of the caribou in. Newfoundland—and I believe that there are still enormous numbers of these animals in existence—probably never see a human being, either in their summer haunts to the north of the railway or on their winter feeding grounds to the south.

On the night of my arrival at Howley I slept at the station, and the following morning, after an early breakfast by lamplight, started with my guide eastwards along the railway in order to take up a position on a good "lead " as early as possible.

As it grew light we found the face of the land enshrouded in so thick a mist that a caribou would have been invisible at a distance of fifty yards. So dense was this mist that, when a little later I was sitting on a large stone on a piece of rising ground, whence, had the weather been clear, I should have commanded a view over an extensive stretch of open boggy ground, a peregrine falcon all but perched on my head. I saw a large bird flying through the mist straight towards me, and did not move until it was close to my face. Then I saw it was a peregrine falcon, and at the same time it realized that I was not a part of the rock on which I was sitting. It checked itself suddenly in its flight, rose just above my head, and passed on, but I feel sure it had intended to perch on my head.

The mist now began to clear, and my guide said we had better go a little farther up the line and take up a position for the day on a very good "lead" he knew of. We soon passed two hunting camps, all the occupants of which were already out watching " leads." When we were some three miles from Howley Station we left the line and turned northwards along some open ridges intersected by boggy valleys. After having walked about a mile in this direction we sat down at the foot of a large pine tree.

The mist was now clearing fast, and we were presently able to distinguish objects at some distance. The first living things we saw were not caribou, but three men watching for those animals on the same "lead" as ourselves, and within two hundred yards of us. My guide swore softly, and I found it difficult to express adequately my own feelings.

We then walked up to our competitors, who proved to be natives of the island looking for meat; they were all known to my guide. Two of them were armed with muzzle-loading weapons, one of which was a long 8-bore sealing gun, loaded with slugs. The third carried a good breech-loading rifle. After a short talk with these men it was arranged that my guide and I should go a little farther on down the main "lead " and allow everything to pass but a stag with a good head.

We therefore took up a second position on the top of another ridge some three hundred yards farther on. Here we sat until about one o'clock without seeing or hearing anything. By this time the mist had entirely cleared off and it was a bright, sunny day.

Suddenly we heard a shot not very far away to the left. "That's someone on the next 'lead,'" said my guide; "Now look out, as the deer may come this way." Some two minutes later I saw about twenty caribou—all does and fawns, so far as I could make out—come trotting into the open and make directly towards the three gunners behind us. I saw two of these men run towards the deer and then sit down and fire into them without

THE AUTHOR'S CAMP NEAR HOWLEY.
Photograph by S.H. PARSONS

visible effect as they trotted past. Soon we saw another herd of does, followed by a stag, coming straight towards where we were sitting; but the man with the rifle ran in and fired at them when they were still some four hundred yards away from us. They then disappeared in the hollow behind the next ridge to the one on which we had taken our stand.

In a few minutes the does reappeared, coming straight towards us, the stag presently following at a slow trot some distance behind them. Looking at him with my glasses I saw that he carried a very pretty head, but he was not for me, for a streak of blood on his flank showed that he was wounded. The does now trotted down into the boggy ground below us, and presently came up to within twenty yards of where we were sitting, and then stood staring at us for some time, evidently unable to make us out.

When I say they were within twenty yards of us I am not exaggerating, and my guide afterwards told me that cases were known where several caribou standing with heads close together, looking curiously at a man who kept quite still, had been killed with one charge of slugs fired from a heavy sealing gun.

Whilst the does were looking at us the wounded stag had halted in the bog below, and the man who had wounded him fired at him again from the ridge behind and broke his neck. He fell dead within a hundred and fifty yards of where we were sitting. He was a fine animal, with a very pretty and symmetrical head of thirty-seven points, both brow antlers being well developed.

I must say that I felt thoroughly disgusted with the whole business. In the first place to sit on one spot for hours lying in wait for game is not hunting, and although under favourable conditions it may be a deadly way of killing caribou, it is not a form of sport which would appeal to me under any circumstances, but when pursued in competition with, and in the midst of, numerous other gunners, I could see no redeeming point in it whatever. However, I resolved to say nothing and see the day through.

My guide seemed full of hope and confidence. Holding the horns of the dead stag, he pronounced it to be a very fair head: "But," said he, "we'll get better than that before the week's out," and presently he remarked, "The big stag are only just beginning to come across the railway, they are always the last to migrate south. If we could only get a snowstorm that would move them, and then you would get a chance to pick some fine heads."

We then went back to our tree and watched the "leads" till late in the afternoon. About four o'clock a heavy fusillade broke out a few hundred yards down the "lead" in front of us. We counted fifteen shots. This showed how well-nigh hopeless our position had been, as, all unknown to us, some other gunners were sitting on the same "lead" ahead of us, and would naturally have got the first chance at any stag that came along. We presently saw the man who had fired the shots. He told us he had killed a good stag, and declared he had only had two shots at it, but my guide who knew him, told me that he was a man who enjoyed a reputation for being somewhat inaccurate in his statements. I afterwards saw the head of the stag he had shot. It was quite a nice one, but not so good as the one I had seen shot in the morning. That evening I again slept at Howley station.

On the following morning, leaving my cook and the guide's son to take my baggage on a trolley. about a mile along the line and there pitch camp, I again went out with the father of the latter to look for a good caribou stag. I may here mention that within a hundred yards of where my camp was pitched the cook found the fresh-killed carcase of a fawn which had. probably been shot by someone the previous evening. The meat was perfectly good; and whilst it lasted I was saved from the necessity of killing a doe or young stag for the larder.

As my experiences of the previous day had thoroughly disgusted me, I told my guide that he must take me for a day's walk through the country, as I would not again sit on a "lead" and wait for caribou to come to me. He acknowledged that it was a poor form of sport, but, said that at this time of year it paid better than walking and looking for caribou, as the animals were all travelling, and so seldom gave an opportunity for a stalk, whilst the country was difficult to get about in, owing to the softness of the bogs and the density of the forests.

We had a good day of it, not getting back to camp till dark. The walking was certainly very hard, but I found I could stand it well enough.

The whole country was level and divided into pretty equal parts of open bog and dense forest. In the bogs one sank over the ankle, and often much deeper, in water at every step, and progress was as slow and tiring as when walking in deep soft snow. In the patches of forest the small spruce firs grew so close together, and were so tangled up with fallen trees, that it was a pleasant change to break through into the open and plunge into a deep bog again. In the course of the day we came upon a fawn wandering disconsolately around all by itself, its mother having doubtless been shot, and later on four does and a fawn passed close to us, travelling due south towards the railway line. Of these does three were hornless, but the fourth had small horns.

The ease and rapidity with which these animals traversed a stretch of open marsh whilst we watched them were most remarkable. They seemed to glide over the surface without sinking in at all, and got along so quickly that no human being, I imagine, could have overtaken them, for in the wet bogs of Newfoundland you cannot run, and may rather be said to wade than to walk.

28

CARIBOU SWIMMING ACROSS A
LAKE IN NEWFOUNDLAND.
Photograph by S.H. PARSONS

Neither horse, ox, nor ass can traverse these marshes at all, as they sink in and get bogged immediately, but the feet of the caribou are specially adapted for walking in soft ground, as not only can the broad, rounded hoofs be splayed out very wide apart and made to cover a large surface, but the false hoofs are also specially developed in order to assist in bearing up the animal's weight.

On our way back to camp we came on two caribou feeding in a small marsh surrounded by forest. They were a stag and a doe, and the former looked a fine large animal. I crept up to within seventy yards and had a good look at him. I was very nearly shooting him, but after studying his head for some time I decided it was not worth having, as the tops of his antlers seemed very poor, so I stood up and let him see me, when he presently ran off.

On getting back to camp I found that two acquaintances of my guide had come up from Alexander Bay to try and get some meat for the winter. One of them was armed with. a sealing gun loaded with slugs, and the other carried a good rifle. The latter, an elderly man named Saunders, had killed during the day a very fine caribou stag with a head of forty-one points, not far from camp, just as it was crossing the railway. The horns of this stag, though not very long, were wonderfully palmated and very symmetrical. I took a photograph of them, and they were subsequently bought by one of the occupants of the next camp along the line for fifteen dollars.

On the following day I again tramped the bogs to the north of the railway, but failed to come across a good stag. Soon after leaving camp I met a doe and a fawn, and later on a small herd, consisting of five does and a stag, passed within fifty yards of the bushes from behind which my guide and I had been watching them as they approached us across an open bog. As the stag had a poor head I did not stop him, and all six animals passed on southwards quite unconscious of our near proximity.

In the afternoon we had rather an interesting experience. Stroud (my guide) and I were resting on a stretch of dry sand just below the high and densely-wooded upper bank of the Sand River, a pretty stream some eighty yards in width. Sitting as we were on an open beach, we were, of course, in full view of any animal standing on the farther bank of the river.

Nevertheless, a herd of caribou, consisting of three old does, a fawn, and two young stags, presently appeared amongst the trees exactly opposite, and without seeming to notice us they plunged one after the other into the river. They swam across towards our side one behind the other, and heading a little down stream, got into shallow water about fifty yards below where we were sitting. Here they stood for some minutes shaking the water out of their thick coats like great dogs. Presently, headed by one of the young stags, they waded one after the other back again into deep water, and swam in single file straight up the centre of the river, and again landed on the same side about two hundred yards above us. They certainly passed within thirty or forty yards of us, but, though we were in full view on the open beach, never appeared to notice us.

As the wind was blowing up stream they very soon scented us after leaving the water, and they then showed the same alarm which is manifested by all other wild animals at the smell of man. As the taint entered their nostrils they each made a short dash to one side or the other; then they all stood still for a moment, looking eagerly for their unseen enemies, and then dashed off headlong.

I noticed that when swimming past us a few inches of the whole length of their bodies was above the water, whilst all their short tails were held straight up in the air like tiny sails, the snow-white underside being fully exposed to view.

During the following night heavy rain set in, which turned to snow before morning, the storm lasting till after mid-day. When the cook brought me my early breakfast before daylight, as usual, he informed me that the meat of the fawn on which we had been living for the past three days was nearly finished, and asked me to try and shoot a deer near camp for the larder. Not long afterwards, on looking out of my tent through the fast falling snowflakes I saw two caribou does standing just on the side of the railway and within fifty yards of our encampment.

I at once got hold of my rifle and, pushing in a cartridge, looked out again. The two does had seen me when I first left the tent, and had trotted a short distance away, but were now again standing less than a hundred yards from me. So I killed one of them with a bullet through the lungs—the first shot I had fired at a caribou.

On the following day I shot another—a stag with too poor a head to keep—out of a herd of six which trotted past our tent just after my return to camp late in the afternoon. I gave this animal to the man with the sealing gun, who had just killed a young stag out of the same herd. He was delighted to get two whole carcases, and took them off home that evening on the slow train which runs over the line daily from St. John's to Port-aux-Basques. This train is called the "accommodation train," and it fully deserves the appellation. It travels slowly, time is of no object to it, and on being hailed will obligingly stop anywhere, independently of stations, and take up passengers or deer carcases.

On the evening of October 31st, Stroud and I came home along the railway and took careful note of the tracks that had crossed the line since the snow fell. The snow had now been lying a foot deep on the ground for two days, yet the number of caribou tracks crossing the line since it fell, between Howley

ON THE TERRA NOVA RIVER.

station and Goose Lake, was very small, and so far as we could learn from enquiry at the different camps, no big stags had been seen during that time.

My guide now abandoned his original idea that a snow-storm would bring a number of old stags across the railway line, and came to the conclusion that the autumn migration was nearly over, and that, therefore, it would not be much use our remaining any longer where we were.

To my question as to whether we could not get into the country to which the deer had migrated, he replied that the difficulty of hunting in any district, which was not either ad-jacent to the railway or accessible by water, arose from the fact that in Newfoundland no pack animals could be used, and thus in a journey across country all provisions and camp equip-ment had necessarily to be carried on men's backs. He told me, however, that if we moved to a station about a hundred and fifty miles east of Howley, he thought we could get by boat to a country where no one else was at present hunting, and where there would be a good chance of finding caribou.

I at, once made up my mind to try this new field, as I was heartily sick of the neighbourhood of the railway. We got on board the train the same night, and reached Terra Nova sta-tion at 11 a.m. on the morning of the 1st of November. For this excursion I engaged Saunders and Stroud's son, in addition to the guide and the cook.

On leaving the train we lost no time in packing our traps on board a heavy row-boat, and forthwith made a start up the lake. The day was cold with a strong wind blowing, which pres-ently knocked up such a sea that we were obliged to take shel-ter early in the afternoon behind a projecting headland and lie there for the rest of the day.

On the following morning the water of the lake was com-paratively calm, as the wind had gone down during the night, so we lost no time in getting on the move. Stroud and I left the boat to proceed along the right-hand shore of the lake and up the St. George's River to an appointed spot where it was arranged we were to meet and camp that evening. We then set off on a hunt into the country lying to the west of our last night's bivouac.

After having followed the shore of the lake for a mile or so, we made our way up a densely-wooded slope, which rose to a height of two or three hundred feet above the level of the water, and presently emerged upon an open plateau of level marsh, scattered over which were little islands of forest and outcrops of moss-covered rock, known as "barrens."

We had been walking for perhaps a couple of hours, and were just entering a patch of burnt forest, a veritable wilderness of dead and bleaching poles, when I suddenly caught sight of the white neck and reddish antlers of a caribou stag.

"Sit down!" I whispered to my guide, who was just in front of me but had not yet seen him, and we both squatted at once.

The caribou stag was less than a hundred yards away when I first saw him, and had he been a sharp-sighted animal would inevitably have seen us at the same time. However, he failed to do so, and came mooning along through the dead and leafless tree stems, evidently with a mind so much at ease that he had not the least suspicion that danger and death might be lurking very near him.

I could not at once fire, as the burnt forest through which he was slowly moving was very thick, so I waited for him to advance into more open ground.

I must say he looked a splendid animal, his snow-white neck, with a shaggy fringe of hair depending from the throat, showing up in striking contrast with his grey-brown body and dark face; whilst the red-brown palmated antlers when viewed from one side looked like some curious spiky growth of wood. He soon got into a little more open ground and gave me a very easy broadside shot at about eighty yards, so I put a bullet through his lungs, which killed him very quickly.

My prize was evidently an animal in his prime. Unfortunately, only one brow tine was broadly palmated, and on this side—the left antler—there were nineteen points. The other antler only bore eleven, as the brow tine was a long single spike. However, the head was a very pretty and regular one in all other respects, and I was very pleased to have secured it.

After cutting off the head of this stag and cleaning the carcase* Stroud and I had a long and heavy day's walking through the marshy upland. Soon after midday we came on two young stags lying down. They were very tame, and allowed me to have a good look at them, but their heads were not quite large enough, so I left them alone.

It was after dark when we at last reached the camping place agreed upon on the bank of the St. George's River, but our boat had not yet arrived. However, in about an hour it turned up, by which time we had a glorious fire burning. Although the day had been bright and sunny, and almost cloudless, it had become quite overcast by the time the boat arrived, and before we could get the tents pitched rain had commenced to fall.

On the following morning, leaving our cook in charge of the tents, I set out with Stroud, his son, and Saunders on an excursion into the country lying to the west of our encampment. We travelled light, only taking tea, sugar, hard biscuit, and a piece of bacon in the way of provisions, and a light canvas sheet instead of a tent. I took a single blanket for myself, but the men had only one blanket between them. However, in Newfoundland an abundance of dry wood is almost

*When on our return the men went to get this meat, they found that much of it had been devoured by eagles.

36

"PACKING" THROUGH THE BOGS
OF NEWFOUNDLAND.

everywhere to be found, and there is, therefore, no difficulty in keeping warm with the help of a good fire, without a blanket at all.

On this excursion we were absent from camp for five days, and travelled over a good deal of country. During the first day's march we crossed the tracks of a great number of caribou. These tracks were all going westwards, and, though none were fresh, the greater part of them seemed to be only a few days old.

Stroud fully expected that we should come up with the migrating deer on some open "barrens" just beyond a little lake known as Island Pond.

We reached this lake late in the afternoon, and, leaving the other two men to arrange a shelter for the night, Stroud and I took a round over the undulating rocky "barrens" beyond.

Late in the evening we saw three caribou does, but they were evidently stragglers, as the tracks showed that the main body of deer had passed on westwards. My guide thought that the snowstorm of the previous week had moved them, and feared they might travel too far to the south-west to allow: us to overtake them. This, unhappily, proved to be the case. However, we followed on the deer tracks for two more days, trudging slowly and heavily along through spongy marshes and dense spruce forests.

Soon after leaving Island Pond we got into a country into which none of the men with me had ever previously penetrated, and passing over the high ground to the north of St. John's Lake, came on a fine river running into the north-west corner of the lake. This river has no name, so far as I could learn, and is only indicated by a dotted line on the most recent maps.

It seems absurd to talk about getting into unknown country close to a railway line in a comparatively small island like Newfoundland—an island, moreover, which was discovered more than four hundred years ago; but the fact remains that

much of the interior, both of the southern and northern portions of Newfoundland, has never yet been surveyed, although
it has been traversed in various directions along its chief wa-
terways. But between the rivers there are stretches of country
which may be said to be absolutely unknown—pathless wastes
of marsh and forest, studded with countless little lakes and
ponds, never yet looked upon by the eye of civilized man; wild
and desolate solitudes, at present absolutely uninhabited.

We followed the course of the river I have mentioned for
some distance westward to a point about three miles beyond
a pretty little waterfall. Along the bank of this river I noticed
many small spruce trees which had been beaten to pieces by
caribou stags when rubbing the velvet from their horns in the
early autumn. This fact convinced me that there were deer
which passed the summer in this district, and did not migrate
in the spring to the northern part of the island. On question-
ing Stroud on this subject, he told me there could be no doubt
that a considerable number of deer passed the whole year to
the south of the railway. In his opinion the oldest and heaviest stags in the island would be found amongst this number. I
made a mental note of all this, and determined to act upon it
should I ever visit Newfoundland again.

On the afternoon of November 5th we decided to turn
back, as we then had nothing left in the way of provisions but
a few biscuit crumbs and a little tea, and the caribou seemed
to have gone right on westwards. We had determined to camp
that night at the western end of St. John's Lake, which, however, we did not reach until late at night after a most tiring
scramble by moonlight for the last few miles along the bank
of the river, which was often densely wooded to its very edge.

It was just commencing to rain when at last we reached
the lake, but we managed to put up a lean-to, over which
we stretched our flimsy bit of sail-cloth. Soon, however, the

flood-gates of heaven seemed to have opened, as the rain, which had at first been light, became a steady downpour, and never stopped for one instant till two o'clock the following afternoon.

I have experienced much heavier rain in tropical countries in the shape of storms which did not last long, but only once before have I known a steady downpour to be so long-continued.

We made no attempt to sleep, as the rain beat into the front of our shelter, and the old canvas tarpaulin leaked so much that it was impossible to lie down without exposing one-self to the drippings from many places. Fortunately all round our camp there was an inexhaustible supply of fuel in the shape both of standing and fallen trees, and by constantly piling great logs, a foot in diameter, on the fire, we kept it going. We still had a little tea and a few crumbs of broken biscuit left, and so were not very badly off after all.

On the following day we were unable to move and had scarcely anything to eat—nothing, in fact, but a small ration of biscuit—as we thought it advisable to keep a little in reserve. As long as the rain lasted we occupied our time in chopping down dead trees and keeping the fire going, but as soon as the weather cleared, as it did early in the afternoon, we set to work to dry our things, and by nightfall had everything comfortable once more.

The clouds had by this time completely disappeared, and the moon, now nearly at the full, was shining softly over forest, lake, and river. During the night there was a hard frost, and the next day—November 7th—was beautifully bright and fine. We made an early start, and getting on to the high ground as soon as possible—since all the low lands near the lake were deeply flooded—walked steadily all day. When the sun went down we were not more than ten miles distant from our camp, so we pushed on by moonlight and got in soon after

THE NAMELESS WATERFALL ON
THE TERRA NOVA RIVER.

ten o'clock. We had certainly walked a good many hours, but could not have covered any great distance as our pace across the bogs had necessarily been slow.

We made two halts during the day, one in the morning to eat some delicious berries which we found growing in profusion on a mossy "barren," and the second in the afternoon to roast and eat three willow grouse which I had shot with my rifle.

The above-mentioned berries are known in Newfoundland as partridge berries—partridge being the local name for willow grouse. I thought them most delicious and made a good meal off them.

The willow grouse allowed me to walk up to within ten yards of them as they sat on the ground, and I shot them, one after the other, through the head. This may possibly be considered an unsportsmanlike action, but, after all, these birds were not shot for sport but for use, as my companions and I were really hungry.

The birds which I shot were almost entirely white, and in a very short time would have assumed their full winter plumage. In the summer their general colour on the head, neck, and upper parts is yellowish-brown, the flight-feathers alone remaining white.

On reaching our former camping place we found that the tents had been shifted to a higher piece of ground, and we soon learnt from the cook, who had been left in charge, that the river had risen so high immediately after the great rain that it had overflowed its banks and converted the ground on which our tents had been pitched into a lake. Fortunately our cook was equal to the occasion, and very sensibly transferred all our belongings, including the tents, to the boat.

I still had a sufficient supply of provisions for another week's trip, but came to the conclusion that it was scarcely worth while undertaking it, since Stroud gave it as his opinion that, with the exception of a few stragglers, all the caribou had travelled so far to the southwest that we should not be able to come up with them. He told me that at this time of year they were accustomed to resort to the thick forests, in which it was very difficult to find them, and that they would not frequent the open country again until mid-winter.

At that time the snow lies deep over the whole island except on the exposed, wind-swept "barrens." On these bleak wastes the caribou congregate, to feed on the white moss with which the ground is covered. In very hard winters they are said to live entirely on another kind of moss, which grows plentifully on the spruce firs.

As the chances of success seemed so small, and my absence from home had already been somewhat more prolonged than I had anticipated, I decided to rest satisfied with the experience I had gained on this, my first essay at caribou hunting, and to endeavour to turn it to account the following year. I had taken out a license which entitled me to shoot five caribou stags and two does, and I had had ample opportunity to shoot this number of animals. But it was not quantity but quality I wanted, and I had actually only fired three shots—all very easy ones—and killed one good stag for his head and a doe and a young stag for meat.

On November 9th I got back to Terra Nova station, and, taking the next train to Port-aux-Basques, crossed at once to the mainland and returned to England via New York.

Before quitting my companions I made arrangements for another hunt in the early autumn of the following year. Stroud was unable to undertake to go with me, as he was already engaged for the next fishing season and the early hunting in September.

Old Saunders, however, a quiet tireless hardworking man, always willing and cheerful, and to whom I had taken a great liking, agreed to accompany me and to find another good man.

Our plan was to get to St. John's Lake by canoe in September and to hunt the country

beyond in the hope of finding some of the big old stags which had passed the summer in that part of the island.

How I fared on this second quest after a fine caribou head will be related in the following chapter.

A WONDERFUL HEAD.

CHAPTER III.

BEYOND ST. JOHN'S LAKE. A WELL STOCKED HUNTING GROUND.

ON THE AFTERNOON of Saturday, September 7th, 1901, I landed at St. John's, Newfoundland, after a passage, the dull monotony of which was only relieved by the sight of some fine icebergs.

The following day, Sunday, was a day of rest, but during Monday I took out my hunting license and bought all necessary stores and camp equipment for a three weeks' excursion after caribou. I then telegraphed to Saunders—with whom I had been in touch by letter since the previous autumn—to meet me at Terra Nova station, and got away the same evening in the slow or "accommodation " train. In addition to the provisions and cooking gear, which I bought locally, I carried with me a light waterproof tarpaulin, ten feet by fourteen feet and weighing seventeen pounds, a sixteen-foot Canadian basswood canoe, and an American collapsible canoe. Both these canoes did me yeoman's service, and without them I could not possibly have reached the country in which I wished to hunt.

CARIBOU IN MIGRATION.
Photograph by S.H. PARSONS

A tarpaulin, in a country like Newfoundland, where forests of spruce and birch everywhere abound, I consider preferable in every way to a tent, especially in the matter of weight and portability. A lean-to made of light saplings, resting on a cross-pole fixed on two convenient trees, can always be put up in a few minutes, and over this framework the tarpaulin is stretched. A fire—as large or as small as you like—is lighted in front, which keeps the interior of the bivouac warm and dry, green spruce boughs are cut to lie on, and there is plenty of room, not only for several men, but also for stores and baggage of all kinds besides.

Day was just breaking on the morning of September 10th, when—after a most uncomfortable night in that wretched "go-as-you-please" or "accommodation" train, already several hours late on schedule time, I reached Terra Nova station. Old Robert Saunders was there ready waiting for me, and after a hearty handshake introduced me to the man he had brought with him for the trip, a fine young Newfoundlander named John Wells.

We lost no time in setting to work to get everything ready for our journey, and within an hour we had both canoes floating on the lake just below the station, with all our baggage packed aboard them. Saunders and I took the Canadian canoe—a most beautiful little craft, very strongly but, at the same time, lightly built—whilst Wells paddled the American, sitting amidships and using the long double paddle, like an Esquimaux in his "kayak."

It was just six o'clock when we said goodbye to the station master and paddled away up the lake. The weather was bright and clear, and the air felt fresh and exhilarating, as there had been a light frost during the night.

My companions were delighted with the canoes, and full of hope and confidence that with their help we should be able to reach a country where little or no hunting had been done, at any rate, of late years—and where, if, as my previous year's experiences had given me every reason to believe, a certain number of caribou were accustomed to live the whole year round, I might hope to meet with some fine old stags.

After a couple of hours' paddling we halted for breakfast, and whilst that meal was being prepared I put a light fishing-rod together that I had brought with me, and caught four nice trout. These fish must have averaged nearly a pound a piece in weight, and two of them were fried in bacon on the spot, the other two being reserved for dinner. They were most delicious.

The fishing season for salmon and trout closes in Newfoundland on September 10th, but I believe it is considered allowable for a traveller to catch a few fish for the pot after the fishing season has legally closed. Until I got some caribou meat to eat I constantly tried to do so, but, curiously enough, I never got another fish to look at the bait which at first had appeared to be so attractive.

Instead of following the western shore of Terra Nova Lake, as we had done the previous year, when we ascended the St. George's River, we now made for the mouth of the Southwest River, which enters the lake at its extreme southern end.

By the time we had finished breakfast a strong wind had sprung up, against which we made headway only with the greatest difficulty, as it blew right in our teeth and knocked up a short, choppy sea. We were obliged to work along the shore for fear of being capsized, and were continually compelled to land, unload the canoes, and then turn them upside down to get rid of the water they had shipped. Early in the afternoon a heavy storm of rain swept over the lake, accompanied by thunder and a gale of wind. This, however, did not last long, and as soon as it was over the wind commenced to drop rapidly, and before long the sun was again shining brightly in a clear sky.

It was four o'clock when we at last entered the mouth of the South-west River, the water in which Saunders declared to be lower than he had ever seen it before—the natural result of an exceptionally dry summer. After paddling up the river for an hour or so we came to a section of it which perhaps could hardly be called a rapid, but through which it was impossible to paddle, as for a space of three hundred yards the bed of the river was studded with rocks, amongst which the water rushed at a great rate. With the help of ropes and paddles, Saunders and Wells—often wading themselves in water above their knees—got the canoes safely through all obstructions, and soon afterwards we camped.

When the day broke the following morning the mist in the valley of the river was so dense that one could not see ten yards in any direction. By six o'clock, however, it had cleared a good deal, so we packed our canoes and got under way. We had not paddled more than a hundred yards when I saw two large objects moving through the mist, not far away on our left front. It was impossible to tell what they were; but as soon as I had convinced myself that they were moving I called Saunders's attention to them, and he at once said that they must be deer. They were travelling westwards and following the course of the river, which here (as we afterwards found, but could not then see on account of the mist) skirted an open tract of marshy ground.

I now landed on the near side of the river and made my way as quickly as possible across a bend in its course, in the hope of getting ahead of the caribou and obtaining a shot at one of them as they passed along on the other side of the river. I was too late, however, as I had not reckoned upon an obstacle in the shape of a mass of debris, washed down by the last spring floods and composed of dry sticks and poles of all sizes. In spite of my utmost precautions I found it impossible to pass this barrier without making some noise, and this must have alarmed the caribou, as when I sighted them again they had already passed the spot where I had hoped to get a shot at them and were trotting along the water's edge, and—as I discovered when the mist cleared off—were already two hundred yards away from me. I thought they were nearer, for although their forms were somewhat ill-defined in the mist, I could see that the hindmost animal carried horns of some size, and was therefore a stag. I lost no time in firing at him and heard my bullet hit. He ran on a short distance and then stood still, evidently facing right away from me, as I could only see the white of his hindquarters.

My second shot missed its mark, I think, for although it hit somewhere, the sound was not convincing, and I fancy it struck the bank just in front of the stag. At any rate, he turned round immediately and came galloping back towards me along the water's edge. When nearly opposite he ran knee-deep into the water, and as I thought he was going to swim across to my side of the river I did not fire at him when he halted. For a few moments he stood nearly broadside on, within easy shot. Possibly he scented me, though there appeared to be no breath of wind stirring. At any rate, he turned suddenly and made for the bank again.

I had been holding my rifle trained on to him for some seconds, and as he turned I still had a good sight on him, and should undoubtedly have killed him had I got in my shot at that moment. But in some way, since pushing in the last cartridge, which must have automatically cocked my rifle, I had unconsciously moved the safety catch. I tried in vain to pull the trigger, and by the time I had realised what was wrong and had released the safety bolt the stag was going up the steep bank of the river.

I fired just as he was going over the top and I know I hit him, but as he was going almost straight away from me my bullet probably struck him either in the flank or hindquarters.

I now waited for some little time expecting the canoes to come up, but as they did not do so I ran back along the water's edge to call them. I had not proceeded far when a turn in the river gave me a view over the open piece of ground of which I have spoken before as lying between the river and the forest, some four hundred yards distant. Here I immediately saw the caribou standing. He was evidently very badly wounded, as, although some minutes had now elapsed since I last fired at him, he had only moved a very short distance, and when I first saw him he was standing still with his head down. Then as I watched he moved very slowly forward again towards the forest.

At this moment the mist lifted a little, and I might have fired at the wounded stag again at a distance of perhaps three hundred yards, but I never thought of doing so, as I felt sure he was done for and as good as mine. Then the mist came down again and hid him completely from my view. I now ran back to the canoes, and, accompanied by both my men, crossed the river as quickly as possible, in order to follow up the wounded caribou.

We soon found a very heavy blood trail, which we followed easily for perhaps a mile in a very dense forest. Then the blood began to show less distinctly on the wet leaves and soaking, spongy ground. At length we came to where the wounded stag had been lying down. He had probably only just got on his feet again when we were quite close to him, for the forest was here very thick. On rising, the sorely-tried but stubborn animal had not gone away at a run, but had just dragged itself off at a slow walk. We were, however, only able to follow at a still slower pace, as there was now but little blood to guide us, and we found it almost impossible to detect any sign of hoof marks in the wet, spongy moss with which the ground was everywhere covered.

52

CARIBOU SWIMMING.
Photograph by J.H. BEVERIDGE.

I know of no country where the track of a wounded animal, if there is no blood on the spoor, is so difficult to follow as in Newfoundland.

Finally we gave up all hope of getting up to the stag by tracking it, and spent a couple of hours in quartering the dense forest in every direction in front and on each side in the hope of finding it, but this plan also met with no success, and at length we returned to the canoes empty-handed.

I do not think that this caribou stag carried a very fine head, though, as well as I could judge of it in the mist, it was a very fairly good one; but apart altogether from the value of its head as a trophy we wanted the animal badly for the sake of its meat, and above all I felt intense chagrin and mortification at the thought that I had mortally wounded a fine animal, whose death would profit no one. However, this is the only mistake of the kind that I have made in two expeditions after caribou.

When we again reached the river the mist had entirely cleared off, but the clouds were now coming up from the southwest, and we had no sooner re-embarked in the canoes than it commenced to rain heavily, and never left off again till after sundown. We therefore went ashore early in the afternoon, and pitched camp in a snug spot in the midst of some thick spruce trees. Then Saunders and I took a round in the rain up the river and across some large, open stretches of bog, but we did not come across any more caribou, though we saw some fairly fresh tracks. We were wet through when we returned to camp—more from the water which had poured on to us from every tree and bush than from the rain itself. However, getting wet in Newfoundland matters very little. As long as you are moving it does not hurt you, and after returning to camp you can soon get everything dried again before a glorious log fire.

On the following day the weather was fine and warm, in fact the heat of the sun revivified numbers of little black flies, which I imagined had given up business for the season, as I had seen none previously, though I had heard that they were very bad along the rivers of Newfoundland in the summer months. I found that the bites of these venomous little flies, though scarcely noticeable at first, subsequently caused a great deal of irritation which took a long time to subside.

On September 12th Saunders and Wells had a very hard day hauling the canoes through innumerable rapids, or "rattles," as they called them, and our progress was necessarily very slow. As I could do little or nothing to help my men I went on ahead along the bank of the river in the hope of seeing caribou, but did not come across any. Just at dusk the canoes reached the foot of a very beautiful though nameless waterfall, and here we camped for the night.

The first thing to be done the next morning was to cut a trail through thick spruce forest, round the falls, and past the rapids above them. when this was accomplished we had to carry the canoes, as well as all our stores and camp equipment, along the path we had cut. This we did in three trips, and before midday had the two canoes once more afloat and all ready loaded for a fresh start.

From this point another two miles or so of hauling through a succession of small, shallow rapids brought us to a fine lake, or "pond," as all lakes are called in Newfoundland. This sheet of water, which is two or three miles in length and over a mile in breadth, is known as Mollygojack, an Indian name, the meaning of which I was unable to discover. After the slow progress we had made during the last few days in getting the canoes up the shallow, rock-encumbered river it was a great relief to reach open water once more.

Whilst paddling up to the head of the lake we saw a caribou a long way off walking slowly along the shore. Presently he disappeared behind a wooded point near the top end of the lake and close, as we afterwards found, to the mouth of the river which connects St. John's Lake with Mollygojack. We now paddled as hard as we could, and I landed in the shelter of some wooded islands near the mouth of the river, without having again seen the caribou.

I lost no time in making my way across a wooded promontory to a point of rocky ground on the river's edge. After standing there for some minutes without seeing anything I was about to return to the canoe, under the impression that the caribou must have turned into the forest behind him, when I thought I heard a low grunt just opposite me, and almost directly afterwards the tops of the horns of a caribou stag appeared above some bushes on the farther side of the river. Soon the animal showed itself in full view, and, standing three parts facing me, offered an excellent shot at a distance of about one hundred and twenty yards.

I fired immediately and, as I subsequently found, my bullet passed through the upper part of the stag's heart. It did not, however, at once make a rush forwards, as animals usually do when shot through the heart, but first staggered about and I thought was going to fall. It recovered itself, however, and dashed into the river at full speed until it was chest deep, when it collapsed and died.

It proved to be a fine young stag in splendid condition, the layer of fat over its loins and hindquarters being quite two inches in thickness. Its horns were small and light, but wonderfully regular, and carried twenty points. Had I not wanted meat I should not have shot it for its head, but both my companions and myself were getting very meat-hungry. Better meat than that of a Newfoundland caribou stag, shot when in high condition in early autumn, is, in my opinion, not to be found the world over.

The following morning broke dull and grey, and the clouds hung low over lake and forest. Heavy rain soon set in

YOUNG CARIBOU STAG SHOT ON THE
SHORE OF LAKE MOLLYGOJACK.

and lasted till late in the afternoon. In spite of the unpromis-
ing weather I went out with Saunders in search of deer as soon
as I had skinned the head of the stag shot the previous evening,
but we only got wet through for our pains, without encountering any caribou.

The next day was not only fine and warm, but actually
sultry. After a substantial breakfast just at dawn Saunders and
I made an early start, and passing through the fringe of forest which skirts the lake got into a country of extensive open
marshes, interspersed with rocky "barrens," dense spruce
woods, and small lakes and ponds. The ground seemed ideal
for caribou, and, as we knew that this part of the country had
been absolutely undisturbed since the previous autumn, we
expected every moment to meet with some of these animals ;
but although in the course of the day we trudged many a mile
through bog and forest, and did not get back to camp till long
after dark, we only saw one young stag. I crept close up to this
animal and found that its horns were small and still in the velvet, so I let it alone.

Just at dusk, as we were passing a small sheet of water, a
pair of great northern divers commenced to call vociferously.
These fine birds are very common in Newfoundland, where
they are known as "loons," and their wild and somewhat mel-
ancholy cry is often heard both by day and night. I have always
loved to listen to the cries of wild creatures, especially by night,
but I know of no sound in nature more in harmony with the
wild desolation of its surroundings than the mournful cry of
the loon, as it echoes across the waters of some lonely lake in
the little-known interior of Newfoundland.

On the following day we pushed on up the river which
connects Mollygojack and St. John's Lake, reaching the latter sheet of water soon after mid-day. The stream which connects the two lakes pursues a most tortuous course through a

densely-wooded plain, passing on its way through several shallow lagoons, the connection between one and the other being often somewhat difficult to find.

Whilst we were having our mid-day meal on the lake shore a young caribou stag came out of the forest within two hundred yards of us, and without appearing to observe us, though we were sitting in full view on some rocks, sauntered slowly along the water's edge for a short distance and then turned into the forest again.

Before we had finished our lunch it came on to rain, and continued to do so, though not heavily, until nightfall. In the afternoon we paddled all along the southern shore of the lake, and by four o'clock reached the mouth of a considerable river flowing into it from the south-west. Here we camped in the shelter of the thick forest, which ran out to a point in the angle formed between the lake shore and the southern bank of the river.

We subsequently found that we had selected a spot for our camp which had been a favourite resort of Indian hunters, possibly for generations, as we found steps cut in the trunk of one of three large pine trees, which grew slanting towards the lake at an angle of twenty-five or thirty degrees. These steps had all the appearance of great age, and the tree in the stem of which they had been cut had evidently been used as a lookout post from which to watch for deer. We found that it commanded an excellent view for a long distance along the shores of the lake, and also up the valley of the river.

We also found the wigwam of spruce poles covered with birch bark in which the last party of Indian hunters had lived, some two or three years before the date of our visit. These Indian hunters were, I believe, principally engaged in trapping beavers, and only occasionally shot caribou for the sake of the meat, and Saunders averred that except for them the country immediately to the south and west of St. John's Lake had never been hunted. Nor had it been even visited except by Mr. Howley—a surveyor in the employment of the Government of Newfoundland—and a lumbering party in search of timber who had spent a winter half-way between St. John's Lake and Mollygojack in 1898.

Certainly all the caribou I saw during the next few days were very tame, and showed so little fear at the sight of myself and my companions that we may well have been the first human beings they had ever seen.

When we were entering the mouth of the river and paddling up to the camping place I have just described there was a single caribou doe standing on the shore, which seemed so interested in the unwonted sight of our canoes that it would not move until we had landed within seventy yards of it. Then, as we advanced towards it, it trotted slowly away, but halted and turned to stare at us again and again before finally entering the forest. A number of Canadian geese and black ducks which had been sitting on a mud-bank near the mouth of the river were much less confiding, and flew off long before we were within rifle-shot of them.

The morning of September 17th ushered in a fine bright day, with a strong wind blowing from the south-west. After an early breakfast Saunders and I started out for a day's ramble through what we deemed to be practically our own private hunting-ground. Almost immediately we saw a doe and a fawn coming along the lake shore, and I stood and watched them until they were within a hundred yards of our camp, when they got our wind, and after running backwards and forwards and staring at us for some time finally trotted off.

We then followed the course of the river for two or three miles, when, coming to a little tributary brook, meandering through an open, marshy valley, we made our way along it, and

MY SECOND BEST CARIBOU HEAD.

after a time sighted a small caribou stag, and about an hour later a large one. This latter came out into the open marsh from a strip of forest about two hundred yards ahead of us, and then, turning, walked straight away from us.

I walked after it as fast as I could in the soft, spongy bog, stopping whenever it stopped and only moving when it did. Presently I was within a hundred yards of it, but did not care to fire a shot at its hindquarters, so I kept my distance and waited for it to turn.

After a time it approached a low rocky ridge and in climbing on to this changed its direction and for a moment presented its broadside to me. I took as quick an aim as I could and fired. The stag dashed forward and disappeared over the ridge, but I felt sure I had hit it, though I did not hear the bullet tell. In a few seconds the animal appeared coming towards us again some fifty yards farther along the ridge, and staggering down to the marshy ground below it, fell dead.

It proved to be a very large and heavy animal and was excessively fat. Judging by the appearance of its teeth it must have been very old, but its horns, though of good length and fair thickness in the beam, only carried twenty-six points.

My expanding bullet—a Government "Dum-dum"— had struck the stag just behind the shoulder and had torn a large hole through the upper part of the heart, yet I could not find a single drop of blood on the tracks of the animal after it had been hit, though I examined the ground carefully right up to the spot where it lay dead.

After cleaning this stag and cutting off its head we hunted round for another couple of hours, through what seemed beautiful country for caribou—a land of marsh and swampy forest, diversified by outcrops of rock, covered with a thin layer of soil on which grew a profusion of berries and white moss. Though recent tracks were numerous, however, we saw no more of the animals that had made them, so we returned to the dead stag and carried its head home.

During our absence John Wells had seen two caribou—a doe and a fawn—cross the river a little above our camp, and a large flock of Canadian geese, disturbed by our approach flew up from the same mud-bank on which we had seen them sitting the previous day. I may here say that from the farther bank of the river opposite our camp there stretched, between the forest and the lake, a wide expanse of mud and sand, which appeared to be a favourite resort of ducks and geese, and, as it afterwards appeared, of caribou as well.

I had just had something to eat and was commencing to skin the head of the stag shot in the morning when Saunders announced that there was a deer on the lake shore beyond the river, about a mile away from camp.

On looking through my glasses I saw at once that it was a big stag, and as I could see, too, that its antlers just above its head were very much palmated, I judged it to be an animal worth shooting. I therefore got Saunders to paddle me across the river at once, and we then skirted the open ground in the shelter of the forest. When at length I got opposite to the stag I found that it had lain down right out on the bare ground.

For twenty yards or so beyond the edge of the forest there grew a fringe of rough grass, but when I had crept to the verge of this there was absolutely not a vestige of cover on the level expanse of mud between myself and the recumbent stag, which I judged to be somewhat more than two hundred yards away from me.

It was lying broadside on to me, but with the head turned away, and I lay still and watched it for some time. Several times it lay flat down on its side, but never remained long in this position. I believe that I could have crawled quite close up to it over the mud, but I thought I could hit it from where I was, and I began to be afraid that the wind might shift and give it warning of my approach. So, taking what I thought was a steady aim, I fired. At the shot the stag rolled on its back, but, recovering itself, got on its legs and came running towards me.

I let it come on to within a hundred and twenty yards and then put another bullet into its chest, and this must have pierced its heart, for it made a short rush forwards and fell over dead. On going up to it I found that my first bullet had entered the body too low behind the shoulder.

This stag carried a truly magnificent head of forty points. The number of points, though high, was, however, not its strongest claim to excellence, as the horns were palmated from base to tops, and the secondary "shovels" above the brow antlers were extraordinarily broad and strong, as were all the points on the upper portion of the horns. Had both the lower "shovels"—the palmated brow antlers, which are sometimes interlocked above the face of a caribou stag—been of equal size, it would indeed have been a head of extraordinary strength and beauty. One of the brow antlers, however, though palmated, was inferior to the other in size.

Still, taken altogether, it was a wonderful head, and it was an extraordinary piece of luck that I, who had only seen such a limited number of caribou stags, should have happened to come across such a splendid old veteran.

Saunders was very pleased with this head, and said that, although in the course of his long experience he had seen a few stags with somewhat longer horns or more points, he had never yet seen a handsomer all-round specimen. I at once sent him back to camp to fetch my camera and call John Wells to help cut up the stag. Whilst he was away another stag with a small head came out of the forest and walked along the water's edge till it was just opposite to me. It then lay down on the

MY BEST CARIBOU.

mud within two hundred yards of where I was sitting on the body of the dead giant.

Presently Saunders and Wells came paddling towards this young stag in the Canadian canoe, and it was most amusing to watch the play of its varying emotions as it gazed at the unwonted sight. Fear and curiosity both possessed its soul, and as the canoe advanced it kept alternately advancing towards it and then trotting away along the shore. It let my men land within a hundred yards of it, and all the time we were photographing, and afterwards skinning and dismembering the old stag, it remained on the open mud-flat, gazing curiously at us from a distance of less than three hundred yards.

Towards nightfall the strong wind, which had been blowing hard all day long from the south-west, died away, and rain came on which lasted till nearly noon the next day, when the clouds cleared off and the weather became beautiful.

As I had two caribou heads to skin and prepare I remained in camp whilst Saunders and Wells went for the meat of the first of the two stags shot on the previous day. Whilst they were away I interrupted my work at short intervals, and reconnoitred the mud-flat across the river.

Early in the day a doe caribou made her appearance and presently lay down on the open ground, and later on a fine stag, after wandering about for some time but never approaching the doe, finally took up its position for the day within four hundred yards of our camp, but quite three hundred from the nearest cover on the bank of the river. I could see with my glasses that this stag carried a fairly good head and was quite worth shooting, though a much inferior animal to the monster of the day before.

I now watched for the return of my men, who had gone up the river in the canoes, and as soon as they came back I crossed to the other side, and was soon on the edge of the nearest cover to the sleeping stag. I was, however, still quite three hundred yards away from it, and, not caring to risk a shot at that distance, resolved to crawl towards it over the open mud. This I did without difficulty as the sleeping animal never once looked up, though its head faced towards me, but continued to dream the happy hours away till its slumbers were rudely disturbed by my first shot. This struck it too low, as, lying flat on the ground as I was, I had underestimated the distance. As the wounded animal struggled to its feet I sat up and killed it with a second bullet. It proved to be a fine old stag, very fat, like all the others I had shot, and carried a very pretty and regular head.

I had now shot four out of the five caribou stags that I was entitled to kill, and I was not long in getting the fifth. September 19th was a soaking wet day, rain falling steadily all the time. Saunders and I went for a long tramp, but saw nothing except a single doe caribou, and I fancy that in wet weather, during the summer and early autumn, these animals do not usually travel in the open marshes, but lie up in the shelter of the thick spruce woods, where it is very difficult to find them. In the afternoon the rain came on more heavily than ever, and fell in drenching showers without intermission until after midnight, when a strong wind, almost a gale, came on from the north-west and quickly blew off all the rain-clouds.

On the following morning the weather was bright and cold, with the north-west wind still blowing strong. Saunders and I again went up the river and into the country to the southwest of our camp, and when within a few hundred yards of the spot where I had shot the first stag on the 17th I suddenly saw a doe and a fawn jump out of a patch of forest into the open marsh about one hundred and fifty yards to our left and a little behind us. As my companion and I were also in the open ground and were moving, they, of course, at once saw us and stood looking towards us.

Whilst watching them I saw another doe or very young stag in the bush behind, and immediately afterwards a great stag with white neck and broadly palmated antlers loomed big amongst the dark shadows of the spruce trees. The doe and fawn which had first come out into the open now commenced to trot slowly forwards, but soon stopped, and again stood looking at the strange objects which had alarmed them, while the big stag with its smaller companion came trotting slowly in their tracks.

The old stag looked really grand, and I lost no time in firing at him as he was moving across the open marshy ground about one hundred and fifty yards away from me. My cartridge, however, hung fire for some time after the cap exploded, and when the shot finally went off my sight was off the stag. The report of the rifle, however, did not appear to disturb it, for it never looked round or altered its pace, but just kept trotting slowly forwards.

I lost no time in throwing out the cartridge which had played me false, and, slipping in a fresh one, fired again. This time my bullet sped true, and my second best caribou soon lay dead on the marsh. It proved to be a magnificent animal, with a very handsome set of horns, carrying thirty-five good points and two doubtful ones, with very large double interlocked brow antlers and first-rate tops, the whole forming a head of great beauty and. perfect symmetry.

It will be noticed that with the exception of the four deer which I had last seen; and which Saunders pronounced to be a stag and a doe with two fawns of this and last year, all the caribou I had observed (with the exception of the does, some of which were accompanied by a fawn) were solitary, and I take it that these animals, in the southern part of the island, at any rate, are accustomed to live alone during the summer and early autumn. The last stag I shot, on September 20th, was the only one I saw with a doe.

AFTER THE HUNT ON ST. JOHN'S POND.

In the spring, when the snow begins to melt, the great northward migration takes place, and it is generally supposed, I believe, that all the caribou in Newfoundland cross the railway line and spend the summer on the cool, wind-swept barrens in the northern parts of the island. This I feel sure is a mistake, and I am quite certain that a good many of these animals pass the summer in the country in which I was hunting in September, 1901.

The evidence in support of this is overwhelming. I found summer tracks in the sandy or muddy ground all along the course of the river I followed, and also round the shores of the lakes. Besides this I came across numerous small spruce and juniper trees which had been battered all to pieces by stags when rubbing the velvet from their horns. The branches of some of these trees had been freshly broken at the end of the summer that was just over, but the damage done to others had been inflicted in previous seasons.

It is very evident that caribou stags which clean their horns in the country round St. John's Lake must have passed the summer in the neighbourhood. Moreover, both Stroud and Saunders, who have spent all their lives in Newfoundland, hunting, trapping, fishing, and catching young wild geese, both positively assert that a large number of caribou remain in the south of the island all the year round, never crossing the railway line, though they move backwards and forwards through the vast untrodden solitudes to the south of that point.

My advice to sportsmen in search of good heads is to try and get into the interior of the country to the south of the railway line, and hunt round after caribou, rather than to camp on the railway line and watch day after day one or more of the migration paths along which these animals move southwards in the autumn; for most of the stags with fine heads which used to migrate annually to the northern parts of the island have probably been picked out whilst returning south during the last few years.

There are probably a good many caribou living in the central portions of the southern part of the island which are never shot at at all unless they approach the fishing settlements on the south coast in the winter. It is so very much more satisfactory to get into a country where no one else is hunting than to make one amongst a small army of sportsmen congregated in a restricted area.

Personally, I have found caribou in Newfoundland very easy animals to approach and kill; in fact, I look upon them as the very easiest to stalk of all the wild animals I have yet encountered. The wind must, of course, be studied; but, this being right, there is little difficulty in approaching to within easy range of them. Any small-bore rifle carrying a bullet which expands on impact but does not break up—a 303 bore, taking the Government" Dum-dum" bullet, for example—will be found to be an excellent weapon for caribou.

With the death of the stag which I killed on September 20th my hunting came to an end, for he made the fifth and last caribou stag that I was entitled to kill by the terms of my license. Besides the five stags I was certainly legally entitled to shoot two does, but, of course, as I did not want their meat, I had no wish to avail myself of this privilege.

The greater part of the meat of the five stags was, I am sorry to say, unavoidably wasted. We always carried the best of it to camp, and hung it up in the hope that Indians might visit us, but they never did. All we could do, therefore, was to eat as much of it as we could ourselves.

We brought away with us the hides, all the fat, and as much meat as the canoes would carry when all our other belongings were on board. Two of the hides we sewed together and lashed under the Acme folding canoe, in order to preserve the canvas from damage by friction against the rocks whilst descending the numerous rapids in the Terra Nova River.

Of my return journey there is nothing of interest to recount. The weather was fine, and we found the water in the lakes and rivers we had to descend at least a foot higher than it had been in the early days of September, after the long summer drought. I finally reached St. John's on September 24th, and returned home in the good ship "Carthaginian," which started for Glasgow two days later.

I most thoroughly enjoyed this, my second little trip to Newfoundland. I got off the beaten track, found plenty of caribou, and of the five stags I shot, two carried very fine heads and two others very fair ones, the fifth being a small one.

The wild, primeval desolation of the country and the vast, voiceless solitudes—where the silence is never broken save by the cry of some wild creature—have an inexpressible charm of their own. You feel that you stand on a portion of the earth's surface which has known no change for countless centuries, a land which may remain in its natural condition for centuries yet to come. The one danger lies in its spruce forests. The trees composing these are small, and of little use for timber; but they may be found valuable for pulp and papermaking. If not, there is nothing else, I hope and believe, in the bogs and ponds and "barrens" of Newfoundland, to tempt the cupidity of civilised man.

I cannot close this chapter without saying a word for the two men who accompanied me on this trip. Their names are Robert Saunders and John Wells, and the permanent address of both is Alexander Bay, Bona Vista Bay, Newfoundland. Better tempered, more cheerful, hardworking, and willing men I have never met, and I can most confidently recommend their services to anyone who wish es to travel in Newfoundland.

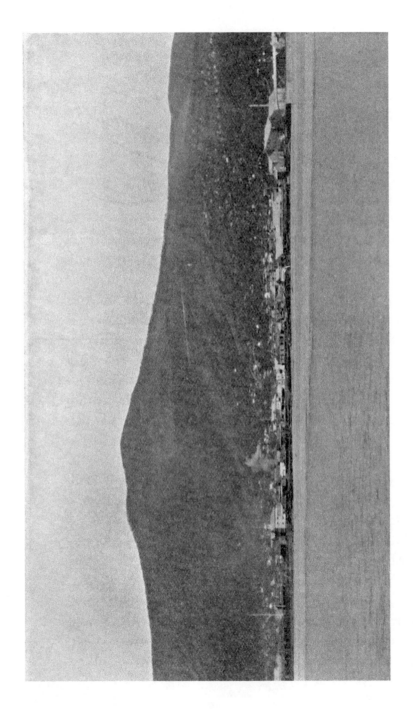

DAWSON CITY, YUKON TERRITORY.

CHAPTER IV.

HUNTING ON THE NORTH FORK OF THE MACMILLAN RIVER, YUKON TERRITORY.

'TIS BUT A few short years ago that the word "Klondyke" conjured up visions of an ice-bound region near the Arctic circle, rich in gold indeed, but girt about with such difficulties and dangers that none could hope to reach it, except at the imminent risk of perishing either amidst the desolate snowfields of bleak storm-swept mountain ranges, or in the swift-flowing waters of the mighty Yukon.

No doubt the popular imagination somewhat exaggerated the dangers and difficulties of the journey to the Klondyke in the early days of the discovery of gold in that region, but that a considerable number of the many thousands of people who flocked from all parts of the world to the new goldfield in the first mad rush for wealth suffered terribly from every kind of hardship and privation, is a fact which cannot be disputed.

Many a poor gold-seeker fell by the way before ever the Chilcot pass was crossed. The surging waters of the Whitehorse and Five Finger rapids claimed many another victim from amongst the crowds of adventurers, who, lured on by the hope of riches to be easily and quickly won from the golden gravel of Bonanza Creek, were wont to navigate the treacherous waters of the upper Yukon in boats and rafts of all sorts of shapes and sizes, many of which were entirely unfitted for such an enterprise.

The romance of the Klondyke was, however, but shortlived, and to-day the difficulties, the dangers and the privations often encountered in getting there, and the strange humours of the social life in the newly-formed township of Dawson, are alike things of the past.

Today Dawson City is an attractive little frontier town with a population of about three thousand five hundred souls, situated on the eastern bank of the Yukon just where the waters of the world-renowned Klondyke River join the greater stream. It boasts a Carnegie library, an up-to-date school, quite an imposing government house, extensive police barracks, and several hotels where good accommodation can be obtained at very moderate rates.

Dawson City is, I believe, something like seven thousand five hundred miles from London, but it can now be reached in ease and comfort by rail and steamboat in about three weeks, allowing fourteen days for the journey from England to Vancouver, four days from Vancouver to Skagway, and three or four days from the latter place to Dawson City.

The voyage up the Pacific coast, should the weather be fine, is a perfect dream of beauty the whole way. The channels through which the comfortable passenger steamers, both of the Canadian and American lines, wind their way between the mainland and the multitude of islands which protect it from the storms of the Pacific Ocean, are so narrow that one almost always seems to be steaming up a narrow river rather than to be navigating salt water.

All the islands and the entire length of the coastline of the mainland are covered with mountains whose lower slopes are thickly wooded to the water's edge. But behind these soft, rounded verdure-clad hills rise great bare rocky peaks, amongst whose lofty crests blue-green glaciers and pure white fields of virgin snow defy eternally the fiercest rays of the summer's sun. I have heard much of the beauty and grandeur of the coast scenery of Norway, and its glories may equal those of the Pacific coast but can hardly surpass them.

After Skagway has been reached the wonderful scenery of the White Pass has still to be seen. The journey through the grand wild mountain-crowned gorges of this fine pass, once so arduous, is now made in a comfortable railway carriage, and from the terminus of the railway at the town of Whitehorse, which is picturesquely situated at the foot of the dangerous Whitehorse rapids, a comfortable steamer takes one down the swift-flowing Yukon to Dawson City. The beauties of coast scenery, the calmness of the Pacific the narrow waters of the inside passage, and the grandeur of the White Pass, are now attracting many tourists to Dawson during the summer months from the American cities of Seattle, Portland and San Francisco. I would strongly advise every Briton who visits Vancouver to make this most interesting and instructive journey, if he can possibly spare the time to do so.

In my own case it was neither the hope of finding gold nor the pure love of beautiful scenery that drew me to the Yukon country in the summer of 1904, but a letter from a Canadian friend inviting me to join his party on a hunting trip to the upper waters of the Stewart River, where moose and bears were reported to be very plentiful, and where caribou and saddle-backed sheep (*Ovis fanningi*) were also known to exist in considerable numbers in all the mountain ranges. I was asked to try and arrive at Dawson before August 15th in order that we might be able to start for the Stewart River by that date and reach our hunting ground by September 1st, when it was thought that the moose and caribou would have their antlers clear of velvet.

Leaving England on July 14th, I reached Dawson City on August 8th, and might have got there four days earlier had I not had to wait two days in Vancouver for the next boat to Skagway, and again for the same time at Whitehorse.

On my arrival in Dawson I was warmly welcomed and most hospitably entertained by my old friend Mr. J.B. Tyrrell, so well known for the splendid work he has done in conjunction with his brother, in exploring the inhospitable wastes of Arctic Canada. I am not given to paying undeserved compliments, but I can truly say that I know of no more fascinating book of travel than "Across the Sub-Arctics of Canada." It is the record, in most simple and modest language, of a very arduous journey of over three thousand miles in canoes and on snow-shoes, undertaken by the brothers Tyrrell in the year 1893, in the course of which the most terrible hardships were cheerfully encountered and overcome.

On discussing the prospects of our hunt I found that it had been decided to try and reach the country near the headwaters of the Macmillan River, rather than follow the course of the Stewart, as the latter river had been a good deal travelled over during the last two years by prospectors, traders and trappers, whilst the former district was said never to have been hunted at all.

A small flat-bottomed stern-wheeled river steamer had been chartered to take our party as far as possible up the Macmillan, neither the boat nor any of the party but as except myself could be ready to leave Dawson before the 18th or 20th of August, I found that I had ten days of weary waiting to look forward to. I spent one day pleasantly enough in a visit to the famous Bonanza Creek, a tributary of the Klondyke River, where the rich deposits of gold which caused the great rush of 1897 were first discovered. I gathered that most of the richer claims have now been worked out, but that a great deal of poorer ground still remains to be exploited by means of hydraulicing and dredging, with a fair chance of making good profits after the initial cost of erecting the necessary plant has been paid for.

As I had heard that sheep and caribou were to be found in some mountain ranges not very far to the north of Dawson, and as I did not see how I was going to get through ten days of inactivity in that town before starting for the Macmillan River, I asked Tyrrell if it would not be possible to get to these mountains, have a day or two hunting there, and be back again in Dawson by August 18th, the earliest date on which he thought our party would be likely to be ready.

My friend told me that there was a trail to a prospector's cabin on a spur of the Ogilvie Mountains, about forty-five miles away, and that he had heard that sheep and caribou had been seen there a year or two ago. He feared, however, that the meat-hunters who shoot game for the Dawson market and bring the carcases in on dog sleighs during the winter, had driven all game far back in this direction, and held out no hopes of success, my time being so very limited.

However, any kind of movement, with even the remotest chance of seeing game, was better than the prospect of days of idleness, in a small mining town, so I hired a pack horse and an Indian half-breed, a most excellent fellow, named Inkster, and having bought a few provisions and a sheet of cotton canvas weighing twelve pounds, to protect us from rain, started for the Ogilvie Mountains on the morning of August 10th.

Of this little trip it is not necessary to say very much. Three days' walking on a trail which was at first fairly good,

CARIBOU KILLED IN THE OGILVIE MOUNTAINS.
Photograph by W. OSGOOD.

but towards the end of the second day degenerated into a caribou path leading through very swampy ground, and which we finally lost altogether, brought us to a good-sized stream much swollen by the recent rains. This was Rock Creek, I believe, and it flowed through fine mountain ranges on whose summits were a few small patches of last winter's snow. The weather was warm but very rainy, and the mosquitoes were troublesome at nights.

The whole country between the mountains and the Yukon was covered with scrubby spruce forest, and seemed almost entirely lifeless, as I never saw the track of any kind of animal, and scarcely a bird was to be seen in a whole day's march. However, we often saw shed moose horns lying near the trail, bleached white, and some of them were slightly gnawed, probably by field mice. Inkster told me that this was a good country for moose when the Klondyke gold field was first discovered, but that the meat-hunters had driven them all far away.

On August 14th we had a long climb up the mountains, and must have ascended quite four thousand feet above our camp. The whole country was furrowed with deeply-worn caribou trails, showing that these animals must once have been in the habit of migrating over the slopes of these mountains in very large herds. Soon after starting, too, we found a fine pair of shed caribou horns, and further on two skulls with horns attached—the remains of animals that must have been killed by wolves or human beings.

A little later I spied a young caribou stag. He looked very dark in colour all over, and showed no trace of white on the neck. I went near enough to him to make sure that .his horns were not worth having, and then passed him to look for something better.

After having climbed to the summit of a high and very rocky peak where I was surprised to find quite recent caribou tracks, as I had no idea that these animals ever frequented such rough and broken ground, we descended to the head of a valley in which a small stream took its rise. This eventually proved to be the head waters of the creek at the mouth of which our camp was situated just at its junction with "Rock Creek."

We had just reached a spot where there was a small growth of very stunted willow scrub, when a caribou stag jumped up in front of us, and ran down to the creek below. I let him cross this, and he soon came to a halt on the other side, and turned broadside to look at us, presenting a very easy shot. My bullet pierced his lungs, and after running fifty or sixty yards he fell over dead.

This caribou was in his summer coat and quite different in appearance to the caribou I have shot in Newfoundland. He was of a very dark brown colour all over, the hair of the neck being as short and dark as that of the rest of the body. His horns which had looked large as he ran were rather of the barren ground than the woodland type, showing good palmation at the tops. They were, however, unfortunately still in the velvet. Had they been fully grown and clean they would have made a fine trophy. As it was I brought them home and gave them and the headskin to the Natural History Museum.

We carried the head and some of the best of the meat back to camp, and on the following day returned with the horse and packed in the two haunches and the shoulders to take back to Dawson with us, as our horse had otherwise a very light load.

On the same afternoon we started on our return journey to Dawson and did not camp till eleven o'clock at night when it was still not quite dark. On the following day we pushed on to within less than twenty miles of our destination, which we reached on the afternoon of August 17th.

On this little excursion I managed just to reach the threshold of what looked a very likely country for sheep and mountain caribou, as another day's journey would have taken me right in amongst some very fine wild-looking mountains.

As it turned out, I might have prolonged my trip for another three days as I had still to wait that time in Dawson before the final start for the Macmillan River could be made. At the last moment my friend, Mr. J. B. Tyrrell, as well as Mr. Congdon, the then governor of the Yukon territory, were prevented from joining the expedition. Nevertheless our party at starting was a pretty large one, as it numbered in addition to Mr. Cameron (the manager of the Canadian Bank of Commerce in Dawson), Mr. Patterson, Judge Dugas and myself, as well as three American gentlemen who had been hunting and collecting specimens of natural history at the head of Coal Creek in the Ogilvie Mountains, and who, now wishing to visit a new district, had agreed to share the expenses of chartering the steamer to the head of the navigable portion of the Macmillan. These three American gentlemen were Mr. Charles Sheldon: a first-rate sportsman and naturalist, Mr. Wilfred Osgood, of the American biological survey, a pupil of Dr. Merriam's, and one of the most competent and energetic of American field naturalists—who are second to none in the world—and Mr. Carl Rungius, a German by birth, but a naturalised American, who is making a name for himself as a painter of American big game, the habits of which he has been carefully studying for some years past in their native haunts. In addition to these seven principals there were our hired men.

The Canadians had two French Canadians and a Nova Scotian, the Americans two men, who, though they had been born in the States, had spent most of their lives in Canadian territory, and I, an Indian half-breed named Louis Cardinal. We also had six twenty-foot canoes between us, our intention being to break up and hunt in small parties after we had left the steamer.

At last on the afternoon of Sunday, August 21st, we left Dawson on board the flat-bottomed stern-wheeler the "Emma Nott," and steamed very slowly up stream against the strong current of the Yukon.

On the afternoon of the following Wednesday we reached Selkirk, which is prettily situated on the western bank of the Yukon, just opposite to the mouth of the Pelly River. Selkirk at present consists of a small Indian village with a church and mission station attached, a few trading stores, a telegraph office and a Northwest Mounted Police Post.

Fort Selkirk was established as a trading station by the Hudson's Bay Company as long ago as in 1850, but was subsequently burnt and destroyed by the Indians of the interior, who up to that time had been in the habit of trading themselves with the coast tribes, and looked upon the white men, not without reason, as interlopers. To their credit these savages made no attempt to murder the white people in the fort but allowed them to return to the coast.

The Indians we saw in the village near the mission station were all living in well built log cabins, and were all wearing European dress. With one exception the men were all very short, though strongly built, and in feature most of them were very Mongolian in appearance. Some of the women, dressed in print dresses, with bright coloured shawls over their shoulders and their heads swathed in cotton handkerchiefs, reminded me strongly of South African Hottentots.

After taking a load of wood on board for fuel at Selkirk we steamed into the mouth of the Pelly River the same evening, but soon getting into shallow water bumped on some stones, and knocking a hole in the bottom of the boat, had to put into shore to repair the damage. We were ready to start again, however, by daylight the next morning.

Our next difficulty was the passage of the canyon of the

lower Pelly, where the river rushes through a narrow gorge between low hills at a rate of speed against which the "Emma
Nott" could make no headway. With the help of a strong wire
cable which was attached to trees on the bank on ahead, and
then gradually wound in on board by the donkey engine, we
at last made good the passage, and entered the mouth of the
Macmillan River on the evening of the same day, August 26th.

Up to this time we had seen no moose or bears along the
river's banks, but this was not to be wondered at as the noise
made by the steamer would have given any animal in our vicinity due notice of our approach. However, I did not notice any
fresh tracks of large animals on the muddy banks, and even old
tracks were few and far between.

Nor was bird life at all plentiful. Wherever we passed
high mud banks along the Yukon, Pelly or Macmillan Rivers
they were riddled with the nesting holes of large colonies of
sand martins which Mr. Osgood told me were identical with
our familiar English bird. I have found these dainty little creatures nesting in many parts of Europe and also in the banks
of the Meander River in Asia Minor, but I never expected to
come across them near the Arctic circle in the wild Yukon
country. We, however, saw none of the birds themselves. They
had all reared their families and gone away southwards before
the 20th August. We also passed some rocks near the canyon
of the Pelly, where a number of gulls had nested, but these too
had all reared their young and gone off with them to the sea,
before the date of our visit. These gulls, Mr. Osgood thought,
were the American herring gull (*Larus argentatus smithsonia-
nus*) which, unlike the European form, seems to go far inland
to breed.

The most interesting birds we had actually seen up to this
date were a pair of ospreys, a pair of peregrine falcons, several
rough-legged buzzards and ravens, and a few mergansers and

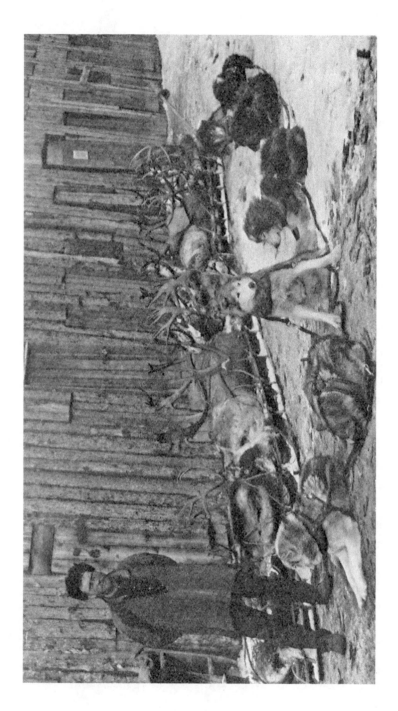

CARIBOU CARCASES BEING
BROUGHT INTO DAWSON CITY.

mallards. Small sandpipers—the spotted sandpiper (*Actitis macularia*)—were very common, running and flying along the water's edge just ahead of the steamer, and I also saw one handsome kingfisher (*Oeryle alcyon*), but, speaking generally, the scarcity of bird life was very marked.

After leaving the Pelly River we steamed slowly up the Macmillan for five days. We found the stream as a rule fairly rapid and the course of the river excessively tortuous, but our greatest difficulty was the shallowness of the water , which caused us a great deal of vexatious delay, as we were continually sticking fast, and often had a great deal of difficulty in finding a channel deep enough to float the steamer.

On August 31st we resolved to leave the "Emma Nott," and proceed in our canoes. Since leaving Dawson we had been favoured with beautifully fine weather, but as soon as we left the steamer heavy rain set in, and we were obliged to camp. As the weather showed no sign of clearing by three o'clock and it became evident that we would have to remain where we were for the rest of the day, I took my rifle and did a four hours' tramp in the rain, climbing to the top of some wooded ridges near the southern bank of the river.

When we left the steamer we knew that we must be very near Slate Creek, a considerable stream running into the Macmillan from the Russell Mountains, where some mining operations are being carried on. As soon as I had reached a point a few hundred feet above the valley of the river, I could see this creek only two or three miles above our camp, and also the point, a few miles further ahead, where the two main feeders of the Macmillan, known as the North and South Forks, join together to form one stream.

In the intervals between the showers I got glimpses of what seemed an ideal moose country, the dark spruce forests being interspersed with open stretches of willow swamp and

THE MACMILLAN RIVER.

grassy glades, in which there were many small lakes. Every moment I thought I should see a moose or a bear, but America is not Africa, and I subsequently found it quite possible to walk for days together in some of the wildest and least-known country in the Yukon territory without seeing a living animal. I reached camp just at nightfall, wet to the skin, but feeling all the better for my walk.

On the following day, September 1st, the rain had ceased, but the weather still looked rather threatening. We soon made a start in our canoes against a very strong stream, and made fair progress by towing with a long line, and poling. The stream was altogether too strong to make headway against it with the paddles.

We reached Slate Creek in about a couple of hours, and shortly afterwards found all the mining party under Mr. Armstrong, a fine young Englishman, camped on the bank of the Macmillan, and busy building a scow, or large flat-bottomed boat, to take them down to Dawson. After a chat with Mr. Armstrong, we all pushed on again, with the exception of Messrs. Osgood and Rungius, who had determined to make their headquarters at the mining camp, twelve miles up Slate Creek, and hunt from there in the Russell Mountains, a magnificent range, whose rugged peaks, new-clad with recent snow, were now glittering in the sun above us. Mr. Armstrong reported that moose, caribou, sheep and bears, were all to be found in these mountains.

Early in the afternoon we reached the forks of the Macmillan, and Mr. Sheldon and I, with our two men, Coghlan and Louis, and two canoes, pushed on at once up the North Fork, leaving our companions, Messrs. Cameron, Patterson and Judge Dugas, to proceed up the other branch to a range of mountains about thirty miles distant, known as the South Fork Mountains, where game had been reported to be plentiful by a Mr. Riddell, the only trapper who had ever been there.

For all of us to have hunted in one district would, I think, have been highly inadvisable, and Mr. Sheldon being of the same opinion, he and I had determined to try the North Fork together, though we had been able to learn nothing about it, except that it was very much swifter than the South Fork, and that we would have hard work taking our canoes any distance up it. We found it so from the very start, and only did about a couple of miles that afternoon before camping at about six o'clock. Whilst camp was being pitched I took a stroll up the river with my rifle and saw a good deal of recent signs, both of moose and bears, but did not come on one of the animals themselves.

Twelve days had now passed since we had left Dawson City, and as yet we had seen no big game of any kind, and personally I was sick of bacon and hungering for fresh meat.

One evening my half-breed Indian servant had borrowed a rifle from someone and gone off up the river by himself, whilst we were chopping wood and bringing it aboard for fuel. Louis passed the night by himself, and came on board the following morning with a fine beaver which he had shot. These most intelligent and interesting animals were very numerous all along the course of the Macmillan River. As yet they had only been trapped or in any way interfered with in one or two places, as the very few trappers who had penetrated into this region had devoted almost all their time and energy to catching martens, which are the most valuable fur-bearing animals in the Yukon country with the exception, of course, of the very rare silver fox.

The work done by the beavers was most astonishing. All along both banks of the river, wherever there were groves of poplar trees, they had cut down large numbers of them. When these trees were small—saplings of only an inch or two in diameter—they appeared to have been cut through with only a couple of bites of the beaver's sharp chisel-like teeth. In the case of larger trees—and we saw many that had been felled which were nearly if not quite a foot in diameter—it would be very interesting to ascertain whether more than one beaver works at one tree, and what amount of work one of these animals can do in a night, for they only work during the hours of darkness.

Along the Macmillan the beavers live for the most part in houses built against the banks. These are large domed structures, solidly built of sticks of all sizes up to the thickness of one's wrist, firmly held together with mud. They can only be entered by diving into the river and coming up beneath them. All through September and October until the river freezes up, the beavers work very hard, cutting down trees and storing up food for the winter. When they have felled a big tree, thay lop off all the top branches and drag them down the bank into the water, and then take them to their houses.

When we came down the river again early in October we found immense quantities of poplar boughs all packed tightly together under the water, and extending in some cases for twenty yards below the beaver houses. Considering that the current in the Macmillan River is very rapid, it is a mystery to me how these boughs were kept in position.

When the river is frozen solid, the beavers live comfortably in the grass-lined chamber in the middle of their wattle and mud houses, and whenever they are hungry, dive down into the water below the ice, and fetch one of the boughs from the store so providently collected in the early autumn. They then gnaw the bark from it at their leisure.

Louis told me that there are seldom more than two old beavers in these river bank houses, with their last year's young ones, He also assured me that in the early spring, before the

NEAR RUSSELL CREEK. IDEAL MOOSE COUNTRY.
Photograph by CARL RUNGIUS.

ice has broken up, beavers will gnaw a hole just the size of their bodies through ice two feet in thickness in order to procure fresh food. Whether there is any truth in this story or not I cannot say. Every white man I asked about it in the Yukon disbelieved it, but, on the other hand, Louis Cardinal, who had a wonderfully intimate and accurate knowledge of all the animals of the North American wilderness, declared most emphatically that he had on many occasions seen beavers coming out to feed in the early spring through holes which they had themselves gnawed through the ice.

Besides the beavers which live along the banks of the Macmillan River there are others living on the creeks and backwaters in its vicinity, and these, wherever possible, build dams which are often of astonishing dimensions. Later on I saw and photographed some very remarkable examples of these marvellous engineering works.

When descending the Macmillan River in early October and gliding noiselessly down stream in my canoe, I might have shot many beavers, as in the evening they often sat on the bank within a few yards of me, and sometimes swam out to look at the canoe. When they were quite close I suppose they smelt us, as they always ended by diving down suddenly, bringing their great flat tails on to the water with a resounding slap: But I had then become a very warm admirer of these extraordinarily clever and interesting animals. I did not want them for food; the value of their skins was not very great, and it would have been a wicked and barbarous deed to have shot one for sport. I may say that we ate the one that Louis shot when we were on board the "Emma Nott." Personally I found the flesh and the tail, which is considered a delicacy, too rich and oily for my taste.

On Friday, September 2nd, the day after we had parted from our companions, we made slow but steady progress at the rate of possibly a mile an hour against a very swift stream,

MOOSE CALF.
Photograph by Charles Sheldon.

hauling the canoes with a line, sometimes being able to walk along the edge of the open beaches, but more often actually in the river itself. We constantly met with great difficulty in getting our ropes round accumulations of drift wood, and in such places continually fell through the logs into water waist deep.

About an hour after our mid-day halt we suddenly sighted two moose—a cow and a calf—crossing the river about three hundred yards in front of us. As we had had nothing to eat in the shape of meat but fat bacon, since Louis had shot the beaver, we looked upon the killing of one or other of these animals as perfectly legitimate, and. I was deputed to go forward and try to get a shot. As the wind was blowing up the river, I expected they would scent me, and they may have done so, as they crossed the river very quickly, and were just on the point of entering the thick forest beyond, when I got within shot of them. I was obliged to fire at the cow, as the calf was already amongst the trees in front of her, but could I have got closer to them, and had I had more time for consideration, I should have shot the calf and let its mother go free, as the former, although I think it was old enough to get its own food, could not have defended itself against wolves, which ravenous animals are said to kill large numbers of young moose and caribou.

When hit and mortally wounded the old cow turned round and again made for the river, falling dead just in the water. On my walking up to look at her, the calf came out of the forest, and trotted up to within seven or eight yards of me, then retreated a little way up the open beach, and then came back to me again. The wind was blowing from behind me straight on to it, and it evidently mistrusted its first introduction to the smell of a human being, as it bristled up all the long hair on its neck and shoulders, and sniffed at me curiously.

I now beckoned to Mr. Sheldon to come up with his camera; but when the two of us were standing together the calf would no longer come so close. However, my friend took a couple of snapshots at it, before it finally ran off into the forest. The moose cow was in fine condition, and that evening we cared not that the meat was tough and hard, but brought appetites to bear upon it, such as the keen air of the northern wilderness, combined with hard work, alone can give. After skinning and quartering the dead animal, we hung up all the meat we could not carry with us on a pole tied between two spruce trees, hoping to find it again and make use of it on our return down stream. However, it was all eaten up by bears long before that time.

CHAPTER V.

HOW WE FARED IN THE YUKON MOUNTAINS.

AFTER LEAVING THE camp where we had got our first supply of meat, we towed our canoes up the river for four more
days. The water was bitterly cold, and when we had to stand
still for any length of time, with the icy stream above our
knees, as was often the case when hauling the canoes round
rocks or woodjambs, our legs got quite numbed.

The weather was at first fine, and the sun quite warm in
the middle of the day, and the midges were then very numerous
and irritating, especially in the afternoons and evenings. At
nights the thermometer at this time registered no more than
eight or nine degrees of frost. As we neared the mountains the
weather became cloudy, sleety snow fell from time to time, and
the water seemed to get colder.

On September 3rd we passed a very remarkable beaver
dam. A backwater of the river, about twenty-five yards wide,
had been very strongly dammed, and the level of the water behind it raised about five feet.

This dam had been carried on one side to the foot of a steep
cliff, but was continued from the other through the swamp
caused by the overflow of the pool above it, for a distance of

LARGE BEAVER DAM NEAR THE NORTH
FORK OF THE MACMILLAN RIVER.

quite seventy yards, in the form of a mud embankment, de-signed to minimise leakage. In the swamp and just on the edge of the lake above the main dam was a very large house, as large a one, Louis said, as he had ever seen. This house, including all the mud and sticks used to form its base, was twenty-two paces in circumference and about six feet in height.

On the evening of the day on which we passed the big beaver dam, we camped on the edge of a willow swamp, in which tracks of moose were numerous. About nine o'clock at night we heard an animal crossing the river.

Whilst Mr. Sheldon and I were pulling on our boots, Louis went out to reconnoitre, and came running back to say that there was a bull moose coming across the river. We went back with him immediately, but the bull had then returned to the further bank. We could see him dimly but did not feel inclined to shoot, as the chances were heavily against any hope of success, and we did not want to risk wounding and not re-covering a fine animal.

On the following day we passed a log cabin in which two trappers named Barr and Crosby had passed the previous winter.

They had evidently trapped some of the beavers near their cabin and scared the rest away, as, although old signs of these animals were very abundant, no freshly-cut trees were to be seen in the vicinity of the cabin.

After examining this little trappers' cabin I could not help thinking what a terribly dreary time its two occupants must have passed during the long, dark, sunless months of a sub-arctic winter. Life on board the "Fram," or the "Discovery," with books to read and plenty of cheerful companionship, must have been quite blissful by comparison.

Later on when returning to the Yukon we met Messrs. Barr and Crosby, and they seemed to be most excellent fellows,

BEAVER DAM IN THE BACKWATER
OF THE MACMILLAN.

full of intelligence, and ready to give any information or assistance in their power to their fellow men.

A few miles away from the cabin near the mouth of Barr Creek, I found a very fine moose skull and horns with very broad blades and long perfect points. Mr. Barr afterwards told me that the bull, to which this fine head originally belonged, had been held at bay one winter's night by one of his dogs, until he came up, and after a great deal of trouble, at last managed to shoot it in the dark.

The dog, which he still had when I met him, was a fine wolf-like husky dog, and Mr. Barr told me that he could rely absolutely upon it to follow up the fresh trail of any bull moose, and bring it to bay.

Once, he said, the dog had nearly got him into trouble. He was going round to look at his traps, with nothing in his hand but a small axe, when his dog suddenly rushed into the forest, barking furiously, and the next moment reappeared with a bull moose close behind it snorting with rage.

As soon as the angry moose saw him, said Mr. Barr, it charged, and struck at him with its horns. He was knocked down, but fortunately not seriously hurt, and on the dog running up and barking loudly, his assailant paid no further attention to him, but again charged after its four-footed tormentor.

On September 5th the weather was very chilly and disagreeable, and we got very cold wading in the river. Early in the afternoon Mr. Sheldon spied a fine black bear on a hillside above the river, and like a good fellow insisted that I should go after it, as he had shot a good many of these animals, and this was the first bear I had ever seen in the wilds.

It took me some time to get up above the spot where we had first seen the bear, and as it was travelling, looking for berries, and there was a great deal of thick bush on .the hillside, I never caught sight of it again, though I must have been very

LARGE BEAVER HOUSE.
Photograph by CHARLES SHELDON.

near it. Eventually it must either have heard me in the thick bush, or smelt my tracks where I went up the hill, as it was seen from the canoes coming down the hill at a gallop. Mr. Sheldon tried to cut it off, but was prevented from doing so by the thickness of the timber.

On the evening of September 6th we had reached a point very near the foot of a fine range of mountains the broken rocky peaks of which rising above the dark spruce forests, which covered their lower slopes, looked like excellent sheep ground, whilst some high bare plateau-like slopes were, we thought, well suited to the requirements of caribou.

Except in the valley of the river itself, the whole country was now covered with new snow, and, as another fall occurred during the night, we found all the trees and the ground round our camp near the bank of the river quite white in the morning.

The mountains were all covered with clouds and mist, but Mr. Sheldon determined to ascend the nearest shoulder and try and find a good camping place near timber line, whilst I took a round through the level country at the base of the mountains. Our two men occupied themselves in making a platform between three spruce trees, and about twelve feet from the ground, on which to stack our stock of provisions out of the reach of bears whilst we were away in the mountains.

I came across some beautiful little lakes in the vicinity of which I thought that I would have been certain to find moose, but the newly-fallen snow showed not a single track of anything larger than a hare.

One hears many tales of moose being seen in great numbers round little lakes in the untravelled parts of the Yukon country. One man assured me that from an eminence he had once counted twenty-five moose feeding in and around some small lakes near the upper Stewart River.

If these tales are not exaggerated, I think that moose only congregate in such places during the summer months, when the horns of the bulls are still growing. In the early autumn they certainly do not frequent such ground, but ascend the mountains and live just on the edge of timber line, and often cross over bare open ranges frequented by sheep and caribou, on their way from the head of one ravine to another.

Mr. Sheldon returned to camp just at dark, and reported having found a good camping place near timber line.

Snow again fell during the night, and continued to do so till near midday, but as it then looked like clearing up, we made a start for our new camp, each of us carrying a pack on our backs. The pack which Louis arranged for me, and which, with my rifle and camera, must have brought my load up to about fifty pounds, fitted nicely on my back like a Tyrolese rucksack, but I found that the straps across my chest rather hampered my breathing when climbing up steep places.

Although I have never been used to carrying a pack, and would not walk along the level high road from Worplesdon to Guildford with a load of fifty pounds on my back, for any conceivable reward, it is wonderful what one can do in this way in the fine vitalising air of the Yukon, without any great inconvenience or fatigue. Louis carried a pack of at least eighty pounds, and did not appear to feel it at all.

Just as we were starting on our climb the snow came on once more, and soon became quite thick and heavy, but soft and watery, and we were soon almost wet through, as every tree and bush we touched covered us with the melting slush.

In these latitudes, the limit of the growth of the spruce and all other trees is something like five thousand feet above sea level, or about three thousand feet higher than the spot where we had left our canoes. A slow climb that with frequent rests had lasted about four hours, had brought us nearly to the head of the ravine where we intended to camp, when Louis, who was in front, suddenly saw a bull moose amongst some willow scrub, intersected by a small stream about five hundred feet below us.

I was walking just behind Louis and saw the moose almost at the same time that he did. Mr. Sheldon and Coghlan were just then some little way behind, so I got the pack off my back as quickly as possible and at once commenced to descend the steep hillside towards the spot where the moose was standing.

The spruce trees were growing rather thickly in places, and I lost sight of the whole of the willow swamp below me before I had descended very far, and on reaching a more open spot, could not see the moose anywhere. The wind was favourable, I had made no noise in the soft snow, and I could not believe that I had been seen. I imagined that the moose had moved from where we had first seen it, and got amongst some trees. However I had marked a tall dead spruce near where we had first seen it, and I worked slowly down towards that.

On getting near the edge of the willow swamp I scanned it very carefully but without seeing any sign of the huge animal which I knew must nevertheless be very close at hand.

The wind was blowing steadily up the ravine, and I was afraid to make straight for the dead spruce tree, for fear the moose might have moved through the willow scrub higher up the stream, after I had lost sight of it, in which case had I crossed the swamp below it would have got my wind and I should never have seen it again. I therefore skirted round the willows just within the cover of the spruce trees, until I struck the stream some one hundred yards above, and as I had then crossed no tracks in the snow I knew the moose was below me.

I now worked carefully back through the willow scrub towards the dead tree near which we had first seen it, holding

THE AUTHOR AND THE MOOSE
SHOT ON SEPT. 8, 1904.
Photograph by CHARLES SHELDON.

my rifle at the ready and stepping very slowly and cautiously so as to make no noise. No doubt the soft new snow and the murmuring of the water running down the little creek close on my right were in my favour.

As I advanced very slowly step by step, constantly sweeping the little willow swamp with my anxious eyes, but seeing nothing, I wondered more and more where the moose had got to. I had at last got quite close to the dead spruce tree when suddenly I saw something white showing just above the willow scrub.

Taking two more very cautious steps forward I saw the upper part of what I at first took to be a pair of perished moose antlers lying in the swamp, for they were quite white in colour. But as I looked at them I saw them move very slightly and then knew that I was within fifteen yards of a living bull moose, which must have lain down in a hole in the willow swamp immediately after I had left Louis and got amongst the first cluster of thick spruce trees. From that moment it had become invisible to me.

Step by step I still advanced until I stood literally within ten paces of the sleeping moose. It was lying facing away from me, but so much in a hole in the ground that I could still only see the upper part of its shoulders, head and neck.

The thought passed through my mind that, if it were suddenly to jump up and dash off through the bushes, I should only get a shot into its hindquarters, which might not be fatal, so raising my rifle slowly I put a bullet into the back of its neck, aiming to reach the base of the skull at its junction with the vertebrae.

The great head dropped to the shot, the mighty carcase rolled on its side, one long hind leg was stretched out with a shiver, and the spirit of this fine old bull passed swiftly and painlessly into the unknown, there to be pursued afresh, perhaps, by the ghosts of Indian braves in their heavenly hunting grounds.

This moose seemed to be a very old bull with widespread horns, measuring fifty-eight and a half inches across the palms. There were, however, only eleven points on each horn. The velvet was still hanging in great pieces on the antlers, but they were quite hard and almost as white as old perished horns.

This moose had recently been fighting, as it had several fresh wounds on the front of its head, which had probably been inflicted by a younger bull.

It was in most excellent condition, with fat quite an inch in thickness over the hindquarters. I measured it carefully with a steel tape, and made its standing height at the withers six feet nine inches. We pitched our camp in the snow within a few yards of the carcase, which was very conveniently situated close to a nice stream of water and a good supply of firewood.

On the following day I occupied myself in skinning and preparing the moose head, and it took me the whole day to make a good job of it. Mr. Sheldon took a long day's tramp over the mountains to the left of our camp, but saw no game and no fresh tracks in the new snow. He found the walking in places very difficult, not to say dangerous, as where the ground was covered with heaped-up rocks and stones, the holes and interstices between them were hidden by the snow, and it was therefore difficult to avoid falling into them, at the risk of a broken limb or a sprained ankle.

On September 10th Mr. Sheldon again took the mountains to the left of our camp, whilst I went to the right, Louis and Coghlan remaining in camp, as we intended to send them: down to our cache on the river with the moose skull and headskin on the following day.

I had not left the camp more than an hour when I came on six wild sheep, two old ewes and four lambs. I was below them, and I first saw just the head of one of the old ewes looking at me from behind the top of a ridge. I thought that there might be a ram behind this ridge, and so walked on till I was hidden by a fold in the ground, and then doubled back and ascended the mountain out of sight, until I was able to make a stalk from above on to the place where I had seen the ewe.

As there are no Indians living in the vicinity of the upper Macmillan River, and I knew that no white man had ever yet hunted in the mountains in which we were now camped, I did not expect to find any game we might meet with at all wild. The sight of me had, however, alarmed the old ewe, and when I got near to the place where I had first seen her, I found that she had walked away with her little flock across the valley below her.

I then saw that there were six sheep altogether, two old ewes (one with only one horn) and four lambs. Having plenty of meat in camp I did not want to disturb these animals, but inspected them very carefully with my glasses.

Five of them—the two old ewes and three of the lambs— were all alike, and seemed to be representatives of *Ovis dalli*, that is, white all over with black tails. The sixth, however, which was presumably the lamb of one or other of the ewes, was apparently dark grey all over the back and sides, with a black stripe on each side of the brisket running to behind the shoulder blade, in fact a typical example of *Ovis fannini*.

Although no old rams were seen on the trip, the examination of the skins of several ewes and young males subsequently shot and preserved by Mr. Sheldon for the Museum at Washington, showed that the whitest looking sheep in the mountains on the upper Macmillan River are slightly grey on the back, and that between these nearly white animals and those of the dark grey *Ovis fannini* type, every grade of coloration is to be found.

I am inclined to think that when a series of specimens of the wild sheep from every mountain range in Alaska, the

VIEW FROM THE RIDGE BEHIND OUR CAMP.
Photograph by CHARLES SHELDON.

Yukon territory and Northern British Columbia has been procured, it will be found that *Ovis kenaiensis*—pure white all over—grades into *Ovis dalli*—pure white with a black tail—*Ovis dalli* into *Ovis fannini*, and *Ovis fannini* into *Ovis stonei*.

Furthermore, I think that it will be proved that all these races of sheep inhabiting the mountain ranges of the extreme north-western portion of the North American Continent, are far more nearly related to *Ovis nivicola*, the Asiatic race of wild sheep inhabiting Kamchatka, than they are to the rocky mountain bighorn (*Ovis canadensis*) and its near allies, *Ovis nelsoni* and *Ovis mexicanus*. These latter are probably the descendants of a species of wild sheep, which came from Asia into North America, at an earlier period of the world's history than the progenitors of the various races at present inhabiting Alaska and the adjacent territories.

After having watched the little flock of wild sheep for some time, I got up and walked towards them. They allowed me to approach within about two hundred yards of them, and then retreated up the side of the mountain. I found that they had been feeding on grass which they procured by scratching away the snow, by which it was completely hidden, and the leaves of stunted willow scrub, which grew in all the valleys up to about one thousand feet above the limit of tree growth.

Further on I crossed fresh tracks of two more sheep, and thinking they might be two rams, though in all probability they were a ewe and lamb, I followed them for a long way.

These tracks presently crossed the spoor of a small herd of caribou, which seemed to me to have been feeding all over the open shoulder of the mountain during the previous night.

As I was well above the timber line, and commanded a very extended view over miles of bare snow-covered ground, I expected to sight these caribou every moment. Presently, however, I got out of their tracks, but still followed the two sheep. These presently led me into very rocky ground, in which I could only make very slow progress, as all the deep holes between the rocks were hidden by snow, so I resolved to leave them and look for the caribou. I was making a circle in order to cut their spoor again, when I crossed some tracks that seemed absolutely fresh, as the soft snow had plainly only just been disturbed.

These caribou tracks were those of three animals, one of them a very large bull. They were heading straight back towards camp, and I had not followed them a mile before I suddenly sighted the hornless head of a cow caribou looking at me from behind an undulation in the ground. She at once made off, and I followed as fast as I could in the snow, and on getting on to a higher piece of ground came in full view of a magnificent bull.

When I first saw him he was standing broadside to me and looked as grand an animal as I had ever seen. The coloration of his head and body was of a very dark blackish brown, but the long hair on his great neck was of a beautiful silvery white. His antlers looked immense and were in fact very fine; long, and massive, and broadly palmated at the tops.

I shall never forget the noble picture that great caribou stag presented as he stood with raised head, and dark shapely form, clear cut against the snowy background. When he saw me he turned towards me, and I at once fired as I stood from a distance of about one hundred and fifty yards. I heard my bullet tell, but immediately lost sight of the caribou, as he rushed down the further side of the ridge on which he had been standing. I followed as quickly as possible, and soon came in view of him again about one hundred yards ahead.

A glance was enough to assure me that his race was run, and a moment later he rolled over on the snow.

I walked to him along his tracks, but strange to say, though the distance from where he had been hit to where he had fallen was quite one hundred yards, not one single speck of blood could I see on the pure, new-fallen snow. And yet where my .375 bore expanding bullet had struck him in the shoulder it had torn quite a large hole in the skin. I can only suppose that the long thick coat had absorbed all the blood oozing from the wound and prevented it from falling on the snow.

Just as I reached the dead bull I saw the cow I had first seen and another fine bull—though a much younger animal than the one, I had already killed—about one hundred and fifty yards further on ahead. They trotted away when they saw me, but soon halted to take another look, and I killed the bull with a shot through the lungs. I now set to work, and after disembowelling both the dead animals skinned their necks and cut off their heads.

By this time it was getting late, and I did not get back to camp till after nightfall. Mr. Sheldon had again had no luck, though he had seen some fresh sheep tracks, and also the footprints of a large bear.

On the following day I took Louis and Coghlan back with me to the dead caribou. The big bull was a very large heavy animal. I made his standing height at the shoulder with my tape line to be four feet six inches. His body was very massive and heavy and as broad across the withers as that of a pony.

Coghlan, who had had much experience in weighing dead caribou at Dawson, said he judged that the carcase would weigh four hundred and fifty pounds dressed, that is, cleaned, and without legs, head and skin. At any rate he was a much bigger animal than any of the caribou I had shot in Newfoundland—as the size of his head is sufficient to prove—and alive I am sure he must have weighed over six hundred pounds. He was excessively fat and his meat most excellent.

VIEW FROM THE TOP OF THE
MOUNTAIN NEAR CAMP.

The head of the younger bull was of quite a different character to that of the old one, as the antlers were not at all palmated at the tops.

I feel sure that the differences between the two heads were due to the fact that one of them was much younger than the other. The horns, however, were so different in character that they might very easily have been supposed to belong to two distinct races of caribou, and curiously enough Louis made this assertion, declaring that the large heavy bull was a woodland caribou, whilst the smaller, lighter horned animal belonged to the barren ground species. Unfortunately owing to the subsequent rapid freezing up of the country, and the necessity of getting back to the Yukon without delay, I was not able to get the head of the smaller caribou out of the mountains and bring it back to England with me.

When sufficiently large series of caribou heads from every part of Alaska and the Yukon territory have been examined and compared, I should think that such local races, as Stone's and Osborne's caribou, will be found to grade one into another, and also to be inseparable from the mountain caribou of British Columbia.

With the exception of the three caribou which I met with on September 10th, no others were seen either by Mr. Sheldon or myself, but on the 17th I came on the tracks of six or seven more of these animals that had passed the day before. Although I hunted round for them for several days I never came across them, or, indeed, crossed their tracks again.

Our Canadian friends, however, from whom we had parted company at the forks of the Macmillan, and who were hunting in a range of mountains about twenty-five miles away from us, met with large numbers of caribou, as we afterwards heard, and were able to pick out some very fine heads. They did not, however, get any good moose, and only saw three sheep—a ewe, accompanied by a two-year old ram and a lamb of a few months old.

On September 15th we moved camp about five miles to the head of a stream running into the Clearwater Creek of MacConnell's survey.

The weather from September 6th to the 18th was, on the whole, very bad. During this time we seldom had more than five or six degrees of frost at night, and during the daytime it often rained hard part of the day and snowed during the remainder. Sometimes a bitter wind blew over the mountains accompanied by fine sleet that it was impossible to face. In the evenings it often cleared up, and during the early part of the night the sky would sometimes become clear and starlit, and we made sure the weather was going to be fine on the following day, but morning after morning we were disappointed.

One night about the middle of September we beheld a magnificent display of the Aurora Borealis. Across the inky blackness of the northern sky a great arc of pure white light was suddenly stretched, which lit up the snow-covered mountains around our camp like a gigantic searchlight, and from the main body of this glorious sheet of flame great darts and streamers constantly shot shivering and shimmering through the sky, now opening out into broad white lanes of light, and again narrowing until swallowed up once more by the envious darkness of the surrounding sky.

These wondrous polar lights were never still for a moment, but. constantly spread and contracted, in ever-varying waves and tongues of light, until they finally died out, and the stars once more shone brightly in the clear sky. Only once again did we see the northern lights, but then, too, the display was soul-stirring and magnificent, and I count these splendours of the arctic sky as amongst the most marvellous of all the wonders of the world. Seen in the solitude of the northern wilderness such visions of glory cannot but awaken reverence in the soul of man, of whatever race or degree of culture.

Whilst we were in the mountains Mr. Sheldon. devoted all his energies to searching for sheep rams, specimens of which he was very anxious to obtain for the American National Museum at Washington. In spite of all his perseverance, however, he could not find anything but ewes and young rams, and had to content himself with a series of the skins and skulls of females and immature animals, which have, however, proved of great interest and value to Dr. Merriam and all other American naturalists.

One evening my friend met with a very curious experience. He was watching four sheep—two ewes, each with a lamb—feeding just above the limit of the spruce forest, on the leaves of some small willow bushes, when a moose cow, with a calf, emerged from the timber, and walked slowly across the open ground towards where he was sitting.

They came slowly on till they were within twenty-five yards of him, but as he sat quite still, and the wind did not betray him, they did not notice him. Mr. Sheldon then stood up, and took a snapshot at the approaching animals with the small camera that he always carried. Directly the old cow saw him instead of running off, as my friend had expected her to do, she laid her ears back, stretched out her great swollen nose, and walked towards him. evidently mistaking the first human being she had ever seen for some kind of bear or other dangerous animal.

She came right up to within twelve yards of where Mr. Sheldon stood, and then looked so ugly—that is, vicious—that he thought she was going to attack him, and he knew that a cow moose can strike terrific blows with its forefeet, and as he did not want to shoot her, he walked round her until she got his wind.

MOOSE COW AND CALF.
Photograph by CHARLES SHELDON.

The scent of a human being seemed to be more disconcerting to her than the sight of one, for she then bristled up all the long hair on her neck and shoulders, sniffed suspiciously at the new and disagreeable odour now for the first time presented to her delicate olfactory nerves, and presently turned round and trotted back into the shelter of the forest, closely followed by her astonished calf.

One evening Mr. Sheldon saw two bull moose. He was then, however, high up in the mountains, and they were a long way off in willow swamps so far below him that it was useless trying to get to them as it would have been dark long before he could have reached them.

On September 17th the weather was still stormy, with showers of snow and sleet occasionally falling. I had been wandering over some open snow-covered mountain shoulders looking for the small herd of caribou whose tracks I had seen on the previous day as already related. It was still early in the afternoon when, as I was looking down into a broad open valley, I saw something move amongst a scattered growth of spruce trees about one thousand feet below me.

I soon made it out to be a moose, and could see that it was a bull as it had horns, and on examining it with my glasses came to the conclusion that its head would be worth having. Almost immediately a second bull appeared, but this latter was evidently a younger animal than the first, as it looked smaller both in body and in the size of its antlers. I watched these two moose for some time. They kept continually butting one another, but only in a playful way, and never clashed their horns together.

As the wind was blowing up the valley it seemed an easy matter to get within shot of them, and I soon set about descending the hillside. Although this was rather open, except here and there for a thin growth of low scrubby bush, I did not think the moose were likely to see me if I moved slowly and was careful to make no noise. I had almost got down to the highest growing spruce trees, and a few more yards of descent would have enabled me to reach good cover, when I saw that the larger moose was standing exactly head on to me, as if it was looking at me, so I crouched slowly down, and then remained motionless. Minute after minute passed and the suspicious animal never moved, but at last it turned and walked up to where its younger companion had been all the time quietly browsing, and both of them then commenced to feed towards me.

I now crawled very slowly and cautiously to one of the highest growing spruce trees, and saw that the moose were not more than two hundred yards away from me. I crawled fifty yards nearer, and was just getting into position for a sitting shot, when I found there was a scrubby bush in my line of fire. I was edging slowly sideways to get beyond this bush, when my weight coming on a dry stick it broke with a loud crack.

At once both the moose faced towards me, and almost immediately turned round and trotted off. They made for a thick belt of trees some two hundred yards nearer the centre of the valley, but had to cross a very open piece of ground before reaching this shelter, and before they did so I fired twice at the larger bull, and heard both bullets tell. Then they were lost to view amongst the dark spruce trees.

The ground in the valley was covered with snow, though it had nearly all been blown from the steep hillside above, and the moose tracks were therefore very easy to follow, the more especially as there was a good deal of blood sprinkled all along the trail. At the very moment, however, that I entered the piece of forest in which the moose had disappeared from my view a heavy snowstorm came on, and in a very few minutes not only were all the traces of blood completely hidden, but the footprints of the wounded animal were so filled with snow that it was quite impossible to pick them out amongst other and older tracks.

The wounded bull had been making straight towards the stream, which ran at the bottom of the valley, so I kept on in the same direction, but in a disconsolate mood, for it seemed the very irony of fate that this snowstorm should have come on at so inconvenient a time.

I had walked close down to the creek, and had but small expectations of ever coming up with the wounded animal again, when, to my amazement, I saw it within two hundred yards of me, on the hillside beyond. The snow flurry had now almost ceased as suddenly as it had commenced, and I could see the moose quite plainly standing amongst some scattered spruce scrub. If it had gone only a few yards further it would have got amongst some thickly growing trees, and I should then almost certainly have lost it. It must have seen me coming on towards the creek, but was probably too severely wounded to move, and another bullet behind the shoulder killed it at once.

It looked a very fine dark coloured animal, and was excessively fat. It was much younger probably than the first bull I had killed, and had a bell, hanging down like a tail from its throat, quite eighteen inches in length. Louis told me that old moose never have long bells. Whether they get torn off in the thick scrub which these animals often frequent, or dry up and drop off when they are five or six years old, I do not know, but I believe it to be a fact that old moose never have long bells hanging from their throats. The head which this moose carried would have been considered a fairly good one in Eastern Canada, as the horns had a spread of nearly fifty inches and the palms were broad.

I now set to work to open the huge carcase and take out the inside, no very easy matter with no one to help me. In fact

IN THE MOUNTAINS, SEPT. 17, 1904.

as I could not turn the dead moose on to its back I had first of all to cut off the upper hind leg before I could disembowel it.

I then started for camp but darkness overtook me when I was still some miles away. However, the night was clear, and I eventually got back all right, but very tired, as I know nothing more exhausting than floundering through a willow swamp in the Yukon country in the dark, and I had to get through some miles of this sort of ground before reaching camp.

During the night the thermometer went down to below zero for the first time.

122

MOOSE SHOT SEPT. 18, 1904.
Photograph by Charles Sheldon.

CHAPTER VI.

THE LUCK OF A HUNTER. A BIG MOOSE.

THE MORNING FOLLOWING the day on which I shot the moose, as recorded in the last chapter, broke clear and bright, but soon clouded over, and a bitter wind blew over the snow-covered mountains. I started early for the moose, taking Louis with me to carry the head back. Close to camp we found the tracks of a wolverine on my yesterday's spoor, and, further on, those of a big bear, which Louis pronounced to be a grizzly.

The tracks were following mine backwards towards the carcase of the moose, but soon turned off and went down into a thickly wooded valley, where after a time we found them very difficult to follow, as there was no snow under the trees. So we left them, but presently came across them again, on an open snow-covered hillside. We again followed them, but had not gone far when we spied a bull moose lying down amongst some scattered spruce forest below us.

I crept cautiously down towards it, and as I was soon hidden by a piece of rising ground and the wind was favourable, I am sure that it neither saw nor smelt me, but when I again came in sight of it it was standing up and looking straight towards me with its ears cocked forwards. I have no doubt that it had heard the crust on the snow breaking from time to time under my weight. I fired at it as it stood nearly facing me, and, as it turned out afterwards, hit it exactly right, in the chest, and I cannot understand how the bullet missed its heart.

It immediately turned and ran behind some spruce trees and then stood motionless for some time. As I fully expected that it was going to fall dead where it stood, I made no effort to get another shot, but waited where I was for Louis. to join me.

Suddenly I was greatly surprised to see the moose trot off. Louis and I at once started in pursuit, and very soon almost ran on to it lying down amongst some small thickly growing spruce trees. It jumped up and again made off without my being able to get a shot at it, but we ran hard on its tracks, now sprinkled thickly with blood, which showed up very plainly on the pure white snow.

We had run for more than a mile, I should think, without again sighting the wounded moose, and I was beginning to think that my bullet had either broken up on impact, or had been deflected from a vital organ by a bone, when we again sighted it now walking slowly up the side of a bare ridge. Making a spurt I got to within one hundred and fifty yards of it before it topped the ridge. It then turned and saw me, and was starting off again at a trot as I fired.

I was very unsteady after my hard run, but managed to hit it, as we afterwards discovered, in the flank, the bullet travelling forwards. Pushing in another cartridge I again ran on, and on reaching the top of the ridge, over which the wounded moose had disappeared, saw it standing about one hundred yards away from me.

It was evidently unable to run any further so I sat down, so as to be able to make a sure shot as soon as it turned broadside to me. This it soon did, and I then ended its troubles with a bullet through the heart. On receiving this last wound it did not move a step, but, without bending its legs, fell over flat on its side, just as if it had received an irresistible push.

This moose proved to be a very old and a very large animal, that had lived out all the best years of its life, and after all had met with a better fate than to be pulled down by wolves, the usual end of moose and caribou in this country in extreme old age. I photographed it as it lay, and made its standing height at the shoulders six feet ten inches in a straight line. Its horns were evidently going back, and had long passed their maximum development. They measured forty-five inches across the palms, and carried eighteen points, ten on one side and eight on the other.

We were now at no great distance from the spot where I had shot the moose on the previous day, so, after disembowelling the one just killed, Louis and I made a fresh start, our intention being to chop off the horns of the younger animal and bring them, together with all the fat and some of the meat, to where the old bull lay. As it would then be too late to get back to camp we had determined to collect as much firewood as possible-for the nights were now very cold and we had no blankets with us and pass the night at the carcase.

Forgetting the often quoted and very true adage that "man proposes and God disposes," I now left my camera on the body of the dead moose, beside which we intended to camp for the night. After a couple of hours' walking and climbing, we had just got to within one hundred yards of the spot where the carcase of the young bull lay, when we saw two moose a good way off just on the edge of the timber line on the opposite hillside. Having forgotten to bring my binoculars with me, and as the moose were a long way off, we could not tell whether they were a cow and calf or a big bull and a cow, so I went off to get a nearer view.

THE GREAT MOOSE SHOT ON SEPT. 18, 1904.

I had to dive into the thick spruce forest immediately I started, and when I reached the edge of the timber on the hillside the moose had moved out of sight. An examination of their tracks, however, assured me that they were a cow and calf, so I started back once more towards where I had left Louis beside the stream, close to where I had killed the young bull on the previous day.

Before I got there I met Louis on his way to look for me. He informed me that he had been watching a big bull moose that was coming down the open valley just above us, and that he had come to look for me, fearing that it would get into the thick timber before I came back to where I had left him.

We at once made our way up the valley for perhaps a couple of hundred yards, and then having reached the edge of the spruce forest, commanded a view over a large extent of open ground in front of us—open, that is, except for a short growth of stunted willow scrub. And there, not more than a hundred yards away from us, we saw a magnificent bull moose walking slowly down the open valley and evidently entirely unsuspicious of danger.

His horns, I saw at a glance, were of huge size, and almost white in colour, as were those of the first bull I had shot ten days previously. In Eastern Canada I think it is rare to meet with moose anywhere except in forest-covered country, but in the wild mountain regions of the Yukon territory these animals may sometimes be seen in the autumn on bare open ground well above timber line.

A view of such a mighty-antlered prehistoric-looking beast, standing clear of all cover on the bare snow-covered ground, in the midst of magnificent mountain scenery, is a sight that once seen can never be forgotten.

But it was impossible for me on the occasion about which I am writing to give much time to the contemplation

THE GREAT MOOSE SHOT ON SEPT. 18, 1904.

of the wonderful picture so suddenly presented to me.

A magnificent specimen of a moose was walking past me, right in the open, and well within shot. A sudden eddy of wind might have alarmed it at any moment, and I did not want to take any risks about securing a pair of horns, whose equal for size and rugged beauty I was never likely to see again. I therefore fired as quickly as possible and my bullet must have passed right through its heart as I afterwards found that it had struck the centre of the shoulder.

At the shot the great bull stood still, and reloading my single barrelled rifle as quickly as possible, I fired a second shot, which again pierced its shoulder within a few inches of the first inflicted wound. For some seconds the dying animal still stood motionless, and I had reloaded and could have fired again before it fell, had I not felt sure that it was mortally wounded. Suddenly, without ever having moved its feet from the moment my first bullet struck, it lurched over sideways and fell flat on the ground stone dead.

It was indeed a splendid creature. I made its standing height at the shoulder six feet eleven inches, taking the measurement as carefully as possible with a steel tape. Its magnificent antlers measured five feet seven inches in a straight line right across the palms, with no long straggling points, and were extraordinarily massive and heavy. On the left hand antler there were twenty-three points, and on the right eighteen, or forty-one points in all.

Altogether, it seemed to me that I had at last obtained a trophy worth a king's ransom, a trophy which would have well repaid a journey to the very end of the earth to get. When weighed at Selkirk on the Yukon in the following October, the horns and skull of this moose turned the scale at seventy-five pounds.

I am quite aware that a number of moose heads of considerably larger dimensions than those I have just recorded have

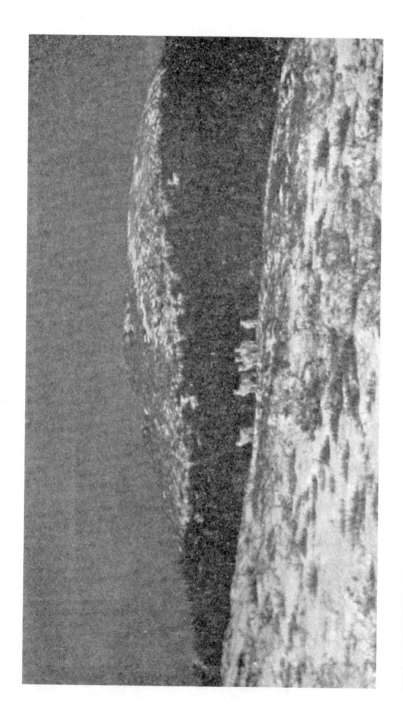

WILD SHEEP NEAR OUR CAMP SEPT., 1904.
Photograph by CHARLES SHELDON.

130

been obtained in the Kenai Peninsula in Southern Alaska, but the moose in that locality appear to be a local race in which the average size of the horns is much larger than in any other part of North America.

My big moose was killed hundreds of miles from the Kenai Peninsula on a western spur of the main range of the Rocky Mountains, and I think I may fairly say that it is one of the biggest and heaviest moose heads ever obtained in British North America, and it is at any rate the finest hunting trophy that has ever fallen to my rifle.

As soon as I had taken the necessary measurements of the dead moose, and after a few moments of quiet exultation over the splendid prize I had won, I set to work to cut off and skin the enormous head, as, had it been left until the following day, it would have frozen solid during the night, and would then have been very difficult to remove.

It was nearly six o'clock when Louis got the headskin packed, and we then started at once for camp, which we reached at last in about three hours, after an awful walk for the last few miles floundering through willow swamps and spruce forests in the dark.

Mr. Sheldon, I found, had again been unsuccessful in finding a band of sheep rams, but late in the afternoon he had located a small flock of ewes and lambs amongst which were two young males. As it was already late when he saw them, and they were in a bad position to stalk, he had left them alone, with the intention of reseeking them the following day, and shooting, if possible, several specimens, including the two young rams, for the Washington Museum.

On the following morning, therefore, he made an early start after the sheep whilst I remained in camp to clean and prepare for mounting the headskin of the big moose. I would have sent Louis to get the horns of one or other of the two smaller specimens of the three moose that I had shot during the two previous days, but I thought he deserved a day's rest and so kept him in camp with me. Coghlan also remained in camp.

About midday I heard two shots which I knew must have been fired by Mr. Sheldon, and shortly afterwards, on looking up the hill behind our camp I saw eight white sheep, all ewes and lambs, coming down a trail straight to camp. As I was busy working at my headskin, and did not want the head of a sheep ewe, but thought the meat of one shot close to camp would be very useful, I told Louis to take my rifle and try and shoot one. As he went up towards them, through the timber just above our camp, they came down into it, intending evidently to cross the valley to the mountains beyond, so Louis met them at very close quarters and killed two, an old ewe and a two-year old lamb.

After he had fired one of the scattered flock ran very nearly into our camp, and stood looking at us from amongst the trees at a distance of not more than sixty yards. It soon, however, rejoined its companions, and we presently saw the six, survivors of the flock climbing the mountain on the other side of the valley.

In the evening Mr. Sheldon came in with the skins and heads of four sheep, amongst which were those of the two young males he had spied on the previous day, the other two being those of two old ewes. These four skins differed very much in coloration, those of one of the ewes and of the younger of the two males being dark grey all over the back and sides, whilst those of the other ewe and the older male were nearly white, though they both had a distinct tinge of grey on the back. They all had snow-white heads and necks and rumps and black tails, but in the two darker specimens a black line ran from the tail up the median line of the body to the grey of the back.

The coloration of these sheep is, I think, very interesting, as it shows that in one small flock great individual variation may be found. None of the sheep found on the mountain ranges near the Macmillan River are, I believe, pure white all over, that is, typical specimens of *Ovis dalli*; but most of them look quite white at a distance, and have only a light sprinkling of greyish hairs on the back. Others again are of a dark grey colour on the backs and sides, and are locally known as saddle-backed sheep. This variety has been called *Ovis fannini* by American naturalists. As I have said before, I am quite sure that *Ovis dalli* grades into *Ovis fannini*, and I think it highly probable that a little further south than the Macmillan River—possibly in the great ranges of mountains south of the Pelly River—*Ovis fannini* will be found to grade into the dark-coloured sheep discovered by Mr. Andrew J. Stone, the well-known American field naturalist, in the mountains of Northern British Columbia.

On September 20th, as soon as we had had an early breakfast, Coghlan went off with Mr. Sheldon to bring in all the best of the meat of the four sheep shot by the latter on the previous day, and Louis and I went back to the carcase of the big moose I had shot on September 18th. I took with me a small camp kettle and a little tea, sugar and bread, and a wolfskin robe lent me by Coghlan, as it was my intention, after having cut all the meat off the big moose head, to start Louis back to camp with it. I intended to sleep myself in the valley somewhere near the two carcases in the hope that they might be visited by a grizzly bear, or that I might see another moose coming down or up the valley.

We first visited the carcase of the very old bull on which I had left my camera two days previously. This we found quite safe, but we saw no sign of either bears, wolverines or wolves having been near the spot. On reaching the carcase of the big bull I first took a few photographs of it, with Louis holding the great antlers in several positions. Then we cut as much meat as we could from the skull, and after Louis had slung it on a pole over his shoulders and started back to camp with it, I was left to pass the time by myself until he returned the following day.

The skull and horns of the moose that Louis was carrying must have weighed nearly one hundred pounds when quite fresh, and as the country between the valley in which it was shot and our camp was very rough and mountainous, with swamps in all the hollows, I did not think he would be able to take it right into camp the same day. However, he did, and I think this was a wonderful feat, as a very large moose head is not only very heavy, but also most awkward to carry. Louis was, however, a very strong fellow, and, on his mother's side, I suppose his ancestors had been used to carrying heavy packs for generations.

Left to myself, I first chopped down a few spruce boughs and fenced in a cosy corner behind the upturned roots of a fallen tree. Then I collected a great pile of dry wood, so as to be able to keep up a good fire, as the nights were now getting very cold. After this I peeled a great slab of skin from the carcase of the big moose to lie on, and then crossed the stream and cut some prime fat meat from that of the younger animal.

Then I took a stroll up the valley, hoping to meet with another mighty bull moose, or to find some sheep feeding on the sides of the mountains, through which it ran. However, I neither saw nor heard any kind of wild animal, and returning to my camping place in the evening, I made myself some tea, and roasted some fat meat on a forked stick over the fire.

I found that the hair on the moose hide was quite two inches long, and so close and thick that it effectually kept the cold from coming through from the frozen ground beneath. Lying on this slab of moose hide, and covered with Coghlan's wolfskin robe, I passed a most comfortable night, and slept soundly until it was broad daylight. I then again made tea and roasted some more meat, and after I had examined the two carcases to make sure that there were no bears about, walked up the valley until I had reached the source of the creek which ran down its centre.

I saw a good many tracks of moose and sheep of recent date in the snow, but did not come across any of the animals themselves until on my way back to where I had slept I spied a flock of eleven sheep on the hillside above me. There was unfortunately no ram amongst them, but there was a very white ewe whose skin I thought Mr. Sheldon would like to have to add to his series of specimens for the Washington Museum.

This animal I succeeded in shooting, and after I had skinned it for mounting, and cut off its hind quarters, I carried these down the valley to my last night's sleeping place, where I found Louis waiting for me. He had got a camp kettle full of tea, and some fat meat ready roasted, and after we had made a good meal we started for camp, and got there just after dark.

During my absence Coghlan had been down to where we had left the canoes at our camp on the river, and had brought back the report that owing to the freezing up of all the creeks running into it the water had got very low, whilst the slack water in the river itself was commencing to freeze. He advised us to give up our hunt at once and make a start for the Yukon, whilst the Macmillan and Pelly Rivers were still open, as otherwise we might run a grave risk of getting frozen in.

As Coghlan had had several years experience of the Yukon country we deemed it prudent to take his advice, as to have got frozen in on our journey down the river would have meant the abandonment of our canoes and everything in them. We should then have had before us a weary tramp across country to the nearest station on the Yukon, and should undoubtedly

136

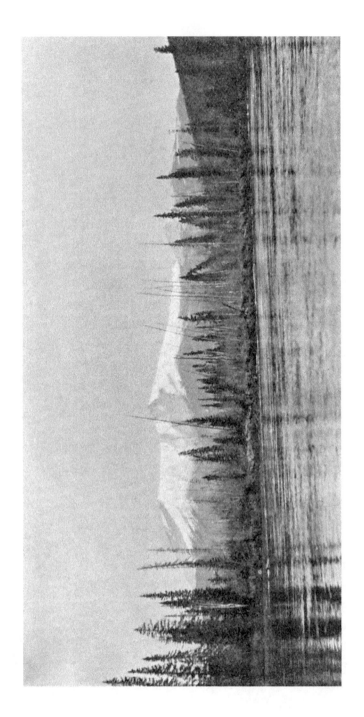

DROMEDARY MOUNTAIN FROM THE MACMILLAN RIVER.

have had to endure very great hardships from hunger and cold, as we could not have carried either blankets or much food with us, nor, in all probability, have shot anything in the thick forests except occasional hares and grouse.

It was a great disappointment having to leave our hunting ground so soon, for had we been able to remain in the mountains for another week or ten days I should have had a very good chance of finding bears at one or other of the carcases of the moose I had shot, and might also in that time have come across another moose with a big head, or a herd of caribou or some sheep rams. However, none of us cared to run the risk of getting frozen in before reaching the Yukon, so we at once set to work to get down to the canoes, to prepare for a start down the river as soon as possible, and in the circumstances I was obliged to leave my two smaller pairs of moose horns behind, as well as the head of the younger of the two caribou bulls I had shot.

I have forgotten to mention that early on the morning of September 20th we saw a fine bull moose coming down the shoulder of the mountain opposite our camp. It was right up above timber line on bare open rocky ground that looked only suitable for sheep, and although I could only get a side view of it with my glasses, it seemed to me to be a very large animal carrying a fine head. As Mr. Sheldon had not yet shot a moose he, of course, went after it, but unfortunately was not able to get near it, before it got down into the thick timber on the shoulder of the mountain, and he never saw it again.

Besides horns and skins, bedding and camp furniture, we had to carry a good supply of meat down to the river for our canoe journey, so it was not until mid-day on September 25th that we finally made a start. On the previous day a thaw had set in, and heavy rain had fallen in the valley of the river though it had snowed in the mountains. This timely thaw raised the

THE AUTHOR "TRACKING" UP THE NORTH FORK.
Photograph by CHARLES SHELDON.

level of the river considerably, otherwise we should have had much trouble, and might perhaps have knocked the bottoms of our canoes about very badly. Even as it was there was not an inch too much water, and in many places our canoes just grazed the stones on the bottom, while twice we got bumped rather badly.

However, on the whole we got along in splendid style and every hour glided as many miles down stream with scarcely any exertion, as we had been able to make against it with the most arduous labour in a whole day. It was the very poetry of travel to be carried thus rapidly down the course of an almost un-known river of exquisite beauty, with a background of snow-covered mountains at every turn.

About an hour before dark we reached the camp at which we had slept on September 3rd, when a bull moose came and looked at us from across the river. As soon as we halted Mr. Sheldon walked to some low bluffs overlooking the willow swamp at the edge of which we again intended to camp, tak-ing with him besides his rifle a birch bark trumpet with which to try and lure a moose within shot.

Just as it was getting dusk he returned to camp as he had heard no response to his calls, and moreover could plainly hear the noise we were making, chopping wood, which he thought would scare away any moose that might be near at hand. He had scarcely got into camp, however, when Louis, who had been getting water from the river, came rushing in, saying that a bull moose was coming on in answer to Mr. Sheldon's calling.

For some moments we all stood listening to the loud grunting of the moose, which we could plainly hear, appar-ently on the bluff beyond the willow swamp, about five hun-dred yards away, close to where Mr. Sheldon had been calling. He and I then went off with Louis towards the sound, and as I did not want to interfere in any way with my friend's chance of shooting the moose, I did not take a rifle, but only accompanied him as a spectator. Just outside our camp Louis gave another call or two on the birch bark horn to encourage the approaching bull, which kept on grunting loudly, and was evidently coming straight towards us.

After a little while it left off grunting, and we all crouched down amongst the willow scrub, watching and listening. Louis then gave a low call close down on the ground, but there was no answering grunt. Suddenly, however, although we had never heard a sound denoting that a large animal was forcing its way through the thick willow scrub, something white and ghostly appeared above the bushes. Nearer and nearer, but without the faintest sound, this whitish object seemed to float towards us, looking like a gigantic moth, till it rose clear of the bushes, apparently within twenty yards of us. Then the great dark form of a large animal, that we knew was a big bull moose, loomed up in front of us, its head surmounted by a mighty pair of wide-spreading antlers, which looked quite white in the dusk of the evening.

There was still a little light in the sky behind us, and Mr. Sheldon afterwards told me that he could see the sights of his rifle quite plainly, and had got a perfect alignment, on the bull's broad chest when it suddenly halted. We found by actual measurement the next morning that it had only been twenty-five yards away from us. It would have come much nearer, Louis said, had it not seen Mr. Sheldon raise his rifle. After a moment of intense suspense there was a loud click, and the moose swung round and rushed off through the willow scrub.

The rifle had missed fire, and my friend's last, chance of securing a really fine moose head—and. I am quite sure it was a big one—was lost. True, he was able to throw the unexploded cartridge from the breech of his Mannlicher and fire three shots at the startled moose as it rushed through the willow scrub, but these were the veriest snap shots, fired more at the sound of breaking willows—for in its flight the moose made noise enough—than anything else, and as far as we could discover, the next morning none of them had taken effect. A more cruel mischance than this missfire I have never known, nor have I ever seen a man take a great disappointment better than my friend.

Had such bitter bad luck at any time befallen the prophet Job, I think it is extremely probable that he might have used language of a character most damaging to his reputation.

One often hears that it is only possible to call up a bull moose by imitating the cry of the cow, after a great deal of practice, and that moose calling is an art so difficult of acquirement, that it has always proved to be beyond the powers of any but a very few white men.

This may be the case in New Brunswick and other parts of Eastern Canada, where moose have become very wary and suspicious, but in the Yukon country where they have never yet been deceived and led astray by spurious imitations of the female voice, I fancy that a bull moose when in a condition of amorous frenzy, would probably come to investigate any noise that even remotely resembled the bellow of a cow. At any rate Mr. Sheldon had had no experience of moose calling and had only taken a few lessons from Louis before successfully calling up the bull, whose narrow escape from death I have just narrated.

Later on when we were looking for caribou on Plateau Mountain, lower down the course of the Macmillan River, my friend approached to within a short distance of a bull moose, which he did not want to shoot as its horns were not large. Having his birch bark horn with him, he thought he would try and call it up, but though he kept on calling for all he was worth for some time and in the most plaintive of tones, the bull never paid the slightest attention to his counterfeit blandishments, and showed neither alarm nor curiosity at the sound. This bull I imagine had passed the period of frenzy which annually takes possession of his kind in early autumn, and had no longer any desire for female society.

The grunting of the bull moose as it approached Mr. Sheldon's call, was very peculiar, and seemed to come from the throat. There was something disagreeable about the sound as it reminded me irresistibly of a human being in the throes of sea-sickness.

Just about this same time, in the last days of September, Mr. Rungius, who had had some experience of moose calling in New Brunswick, called up two bull moose in one evening. Mr. Osgood was with him, and told me all about it later on.

The first moose was a young bull, and came up to the call very rapidly. He not only kept grunting loudly, but continually clashed his horns against the trees and bushes. When he was quite close, but amongst some very thick spruce trees, another bull was heard approaching, and came into full view at a distance of about three hundred yards. He seemed to be a very large animal with a fine pair of horns, but, unfortunately, when he came near and drove off the younger bull, it was too dark to see him or to shoot. Still this was another case of a white man, who could not have had any very great experience in moose calling, succeeding in overcoming the suspicions of two bulls, and luring them both within shot in one evening.

On the afternoon of September 26th we reached the forks of the Macmillan, and here we met two trappers, Messrs. Barr and Crosby, on their way up to a cabin we had seen close to where we had left our canoes, before going into the mountains to hunt. This cabin they had built the previous year, and they intended to spend the winter in it whilst engaged in trapping martens and beavers. During that time they and two other trappers, Messrs. Riddell and Cameron, would be the only human beings in all the vast country drained by the two branches of the Macmillan River, for there are no Indians in any part of this territory.

We heard from the trappers that our Canadian friends had gone down the river from the South Fork, on their way to Dawson on the 23rd, and that Messrs. Osgood and Rungius were waiting for us in an old cabin on the main stream of the Macmillan, near Plateau Mountain. We subsequently learned that the Canadian party had come across large herds of caribou in the mountains on the South Fork, and had shot eleven fine bulls, some of them with exceptionally large heads. They had also killed two moose, two black bears, a wolf and a beaver; but had only seen three wild sheep—a ewe and lamb, and a two-year old ram.

Mr. Sheldon and I might have shot a considerable number of beavers, as we saw several every day all the way down nearly to the junction of the Macmillan with the Pelly River. In the evenings they were very tame, and as long as we made no noise would sit on the bank, watching the canoes as they drifted quietly past them, without showing any signs of alarm. Sometimes they even swam out to examine the strange apparitions, diving down when quite close to us, and after having got our wind, I suppose.

In diving, as I have previously related, the beaver always brings its large flat tail down on the water with a loud slap that can be heard at a considerable distance. This action is said to be an alarm signal, and certainly ought to give notice to all other beavers within hearing that one of their number had dived under water in a hurry. However, on two occasions when a beaver made a loud slap with his tail on diving down close to my canoe, there was another beaver sitting on the bank within twenty yards, which was apparently

POPLAR TREES CUT DOWN BY BEAVERS
ON THE MACMILLAN RIVER.
Photograph by W. OSGOOD.

undisturbed by the sound, as it remained where it was and did not run into the water.

During the time we had been away up the North Fork the beavers had done an immense amount of work, and had laid up enormous stores of food in the shape of the upper branches of the cotton wood trees which they had felled in great numbers. These branches were now packed under water, and extended for, many yards below the houses they had built along the banks of the river, for the most part only just above the water level.

Neither Mr. Sheldon nor I ever attempted to kill one of these beavers, as we had not the heart to destroy such wise and industrious animals. Most of them will, however, I fear, be trapped during the next few years.

The mild weather which had set in on September 24th lasted until the night of the 29th, when the sky again cleared and it became cold. During the intervening six days it rained almost incessantly day and night.

On September 27th we rejoined our friends, Messrs. Osgood and Rungius, at an old cabin near the foot of the Plateau Mountain. Mr. Rungius had shot a fine bull moose at Russell Creek, with a remarkably handsome head, with fine long palms, long graceful points, and a spread of fifty-six inches. He had also shot in the same district a caribou cow with a nice pair of horns, and had the luck to get a bear at each carcase. Both of these were fair-sized animals, the one a grizzly, the other a brown bear.

Mr. Osgood had been principally engaged in collecting small mammals and birds, but he had tramped all over the Russell Mountains in search of sheep, of which he wanted to procure specimens, but had not come across any, although he had seen tracks.

Whilst waiting for us our friends had spent a few days hunting on Plateau Mountain, and had killed three caribou.

WOLVERINE SHOT AND PHOTOGRAPHED
ON THE CARCASE OF A CARIBOU.
By CARL RUNGIUS.

One of these shot by Mr. Rungius had very large but very ugly horns. They measured fifty-one inches from the burr to the top of the main beam, and were very thick and heavy, but with very little palmation anywhere. At this carcase Mr. Rungius had again had the good fortune to find and kill a wolverine with a long shot. The day before we reached the cabin Mr. Osgood had shot a young bull moose close to the bank of the river. Its horns had a spread of forty-eight inches.

It was near this camp that Mr. Rungius had called up the two moose bulls one evening, of which I have already spoken. As Mr. Sheldon and I wished to have another try for caribou, we decided to "pack" up to the edge of the timber line on Plateau Mountain, and see if we could come across any of these animals on its flat grassy summit, our friends agreeing to wait for us further down the river.

On September 28th it rained so hard that we could do nothing, so we all took a day's rest in the shelter of the cabin. The following morning, too, broke in rain and mist, but as it looked a little better after breakfast, Mr. Sheldon and I, with Coghlan and Louis, commenced to climb the mountain, carrying light packs, whilst our friends and Gage started down river in their canoe. As the day went on the weather improved, and early in the night the sky became quite clear. At the same time it became rapidly colder, and before morning the temperature must have fallen to below zero.

On our way up the mountain we came across a very large porcupine, which, as usual with these animals, made no attempt to hurry out of our way, but came to a halt when anyone approached it, and stood ready to strike its enemies with its spiny tail. When one held the sole of one's boot close above its back it would give a flick and leave several short quills sticking in the leather or rubber. These little quills have serated edges, and if they should pierce the skin of an animal that cannot

CARIBOU STAG SHOT AND PHOTOGRAPHED
BY CARL RUNGIUS ON PLATEAU MOUNTAIN.

at once extract them, they work gradually deeper and deeper into the flesh; so that in spite of its slothful movements the porcupine of North America is probably but seldom molested by predatory animals.

During the intense cold of the winter months near the Arctic circle the hairy coat of the porcupine, which in more temperate regions is quite short, becomes so long and thick that its quills are completely hidden from view.

On Friday, September 30th, the weather was bright and clear, but very cold, with a strong wind blowing from the north. Mr. Sheldon and I had a long day's tramp, he taking the right hand beat from our camp and I the left. I took Louis with me, and we first climbed to the top of Plateau Mountain, and, after crossing to the further side, made a long round back over the shoulders, climbing up and down many gulches, and reaching camp just at dark. We found the snow lying pretty deep on the flat top of the mountain, and crossed no caribou tracks at all.

In the evening I saw and might have shot a moose bull with a fairly good head, but I spared it, as I did not want to be lumbered up with anything but a really fine pair of horns.

Mr. Sheldon came across the tracks of some sheep, and followed them a long way to an out-lying spur of the mountain, but failed to overtake them. On his way back to camp he saw a caribou cow with a small calf and two bull moose, both with bad heads, the one only having one horn. It was one of these bulls that he tried to call up to him, but without success, by grunting and bellowing through a birch bark trumpet in a manner which Louis declared to be like the cry of a moose cow.

It now seemed clear that the caribou had left the open summit of Plateau Mountain, and we could not afford the time to look for them on the neighbouring ranges, as with the return of the cold weather it was necessary to get out of the country before the rivers froze solid. We therefore returned to

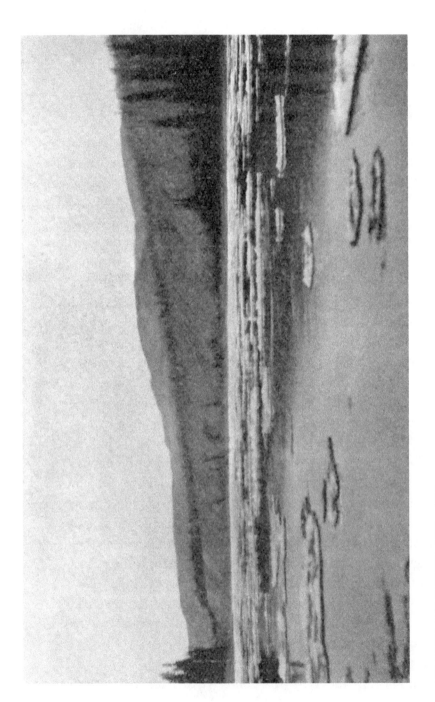

ICE ON THE PELLY RIVER, OCT., 1904.

the cabin at the foot of the mountain on the following day, and on October 2nd once more started in our canoes for Selkirk, overtaking our friends about noon the next day.

The nights were now very cold, and the river became so full of large sheets of floating ice that our progress was very much impeded. On several occasions these masses of floating ice quite filled the river from side to side, and we could do nothing but travel with the pack until we got to broader reaches and were able to find open channels again amongst the floes.

On the morning of October 4th a piece of hard ice knocked a hole in my canoe near the bow, and we had to go ashore and plug it up. The same evening we reached the mouth of Kalzas River, and in the large cabin there found that a French Canadian, named Lebel, had established himself and meant to pass the winter trapping. We here got an old fruit tin, and with this and a small packet of copper nails which I had brought with me from Dawson, Louis patched up my injured canoe most successfully.

We spent the night in the cabin with Lebel, who insisted upon opening a tin of butter for our benefit, though we were just getting back to civilization, and he was about to spend a long dreary winter in the wilds. However, we were able to give him a good supply of fresh meat, and all the flour and bacon and moose fat we did not require to take us into Selkirk.

Lebel told me that he had been born at Rimouski, on the Lower St. Lawrence, in Eastern Canada, and had left home thirty years before, when only sixteen years of age. Ever since that time he had lived in the woods trapping and hunting, moving ever westwards towards the setting sun. On the discovery of the Klondyke goldfields he had crossed the Rocky Mountains and tried his hand at prospecting, but had soon taken to the woods again. He was evidently an

GRIZZLY BEAR SHOT AND PHOTOGRAPHED BY
CARL RUNGIUS IN THE RUSSELL MOUNTAINS.

expert canoeman, as he had poled and tracked* his loaded canoe all by himself from Selkirk up the lower Pelly into the Macmillan.

On the morning of October 6th, the day after we had parted from Lebel, we found the ice badly jammed in the narrow gorge above the canyon of the Pelly River, which we had entered on the previous afternoon. At one time it really seemed as if we would be unable to get through, but fortunately the jam had only just been formed, and the several pieces of ice were not frozen together, and as the stream swept into and through the canyon at a terrific pace it kept everything moving.

In the rapids below the canyon the ice got very much broken up, and between the grinding floes and a good number of rocks, either jutting out from, or just below, the surface of the water, there seemed to be a good chance of getting one of our canoes smashed, but the danger was, I think, less than it appeared. At any rate we got all our canoes safely through without any mishap and reached Selkirk after dark on the evening of October 7th.

On our way down stream from Lebel's cabin to Selkirk we saw a fine black bear one morning looking for berries on a hillside above the river. My friends all insisted that I should go after it as I had never yet shot a bear, but though I got to land without apparently attracting its attention, it winded me and made off over the top of the hill before I could get within shot.

We also saw a wolf, a fine cross fox, and several lynxes on the open beaches near the edge of the river, but neither of the first mentioned animals and only one of the lynxes was bagged from the canoes. This animal fell to Mr. Sheldon's rifle.

Of birds very few species were seen, but every day we disturbed a few harlequin ducks, and mergansers on the river, and saw a few hawks and ravens in the trees along the banks.

* i.e., towed or hauled.

These latter appeared to be very hungry, as when they sighted the meat in the canoes they flew round and round croaking loudly just above our heads.

One day, too, we came on a solitary American herring gull, a bird of the year in grey plumage, all by itself and evidently starving. It followed our canoes for miles until we went ashore for our midday meal, and then alighted on the shore-ice close to us. We threw it some pieces of meat, which it swallowed greedily, and the amount it ate before we again proceeded on our journey would have made a good meal for a hungry man. We left it standing on the ice absolutely gorged, but still surrounded by many pieces of meat, and never saw it again. What it was doing so far inland and all by itself, so long after all other gulls which breed on the Yukon and Pelly Rivers had left for the sea-coast, I do not know.

With our return to Selkirk my pleasant little trip into the wilds of the Yukon territory came to an end. The North Fork of the Macmillan is a hard country in which to undertake a hunt as Mr. Sheldon and I had done, without a guide or any Indian packers, or other means of transport, but as both the moose and caribou grow very large in that district, and bears and wild sheep are also to be found there, it is undoubtedly a tempting locality for a hunter.

The great trouble is the shortness of the season during which it is possible to hunt, for the antlers of moose and caribou are not clear of velvet before the first week in September, and it is not safe to remain in the country after October 1st at the latest for fear of getting frozen in.

Still, whatever its drawbacks may be from the point of view of the big game hunter, I found the Yukon territory a most fascinating country in which to spend a holiday. Its climate is splendidly health-giving and invigorating, its mountain and river scenery superb, and there is still a fair quantity of game to be found in those districts that have not yet been touched by miners and meat-hunters.

THE EXPLOITS RIVER FROM NEAR LLOYD'S LAKE.

CHAPTER VII.

A JOURNEY TO KING GEORGE'S LAKE, NEWFOUNDLAND.

A GLANCE AT any map of Newfoundland will show that in the interior of the south-western portion of that island there is a small lake named after King George the Fourth, out of which there runs a river connecting it with Red Indian Lake by way of Lloyd's Pond.

King George the Fourth's Lake, I was informed by Mr. Howley, the veteran explorer and surveyor of so much of the interior of Newfoundland, had been discovered by a surveyor named Cormack in about 1830, and named by him after the reigning sovereign of that time.

After Cormack's discovery it was, however, never again seen by a white man until Mr. Howley himself visited it in 1875, since which time, to the best of the latter's knowledge and belief, no one else had ever been there.

This does not mean that there is any great difficulty in getting to King George's Lake, but it proves, I think, that the interior of Newfoundland has no attractions for the white inhabitants of the island, all of whom live on the seaboard, and depend for their living almost entirely on the cod fishery,

BEAVER WORK ON THE MACMILLAN RIVER.
Photograph by W. OSGOOD.

and the annual slaughter of seals on the ice floes off the coast of Labrador.

In the autumn of 1905 I paid my third visit to Newfoundland in order to see something of the interior of the island, as well as shoot a few caribou.

The latter ambition, had it been the sole object of my journey, might have been satisfied easily enough quite close to the railway line which crosses the island, but I love to hunt and study the habits of game whenever possible in wild and little-known districts, and I therefore determined to try and reach the lake which Mr. Howley thought that no one but himself had visited since Cormack first discovered it more than seventy years ago.

Having arrived at Millertown, the lumber camp at the north-eastern end of Red Indian Lake, on October 6th, I was enabled through the kindness of Mr. Beeton, Lord Northcliffe's agent, who put his little steamer at my disposal, to reach the south-western extremity of that lake early on the following afternoon. After having had something to eat I put all my belongings into my twenty-foot Peterborough canoe and at once commenced the ascent of the Exploits River (locally known as Lloyd's River).

I had two excellent men with me, Joseph Geange and Samuel Smart, both of Alexander Bay, typical Newfoundlanders, strong, hardy, good-tempered and willing. We got on splendidly together all through the trip, and I never wish to meet with better companions with whom to journey through a wild and somewhat rough country.

Although our progress was slow owing to the shallow-ness of the water in many parts of the river, we met with no difficulties in the way of falls or dangerous rapids, and reached Lloyd's Lake soon after midday on the morning of the 10th without once having had to take our canoe out of the water.

The lumberers from Millertown, we found, had cut all the best timber on both banks of the river as far as Lloyd's Lake, and for two or three miles along the western shore of the lake itself. Beyond that point, however, no lumbering at all had been done, and since the aboriginal Indians had died out, the country had remained uninhabited and undisturbed.

Lloyd's River runs between two lines of hills which rise to a height of between one thousand and two thousand feet, the lower portions being densely wooded. The caribou do not seem to frequent the valley of the river or to cross it in any number during migration. At any rate we saw none of the animals themselves and but few tracks either on our way to Lloyd's Lake or on the return journey. On the other hand, they cross the lower end of Lloyd's Lake, which is about a mile in breadth, and Red Indian Lake, which is some five miles across, in great numbers, and later on I had the pleasure of watching several bands swimming swiftly and easily across both these sheets of water.

Just before reaching Lloyd's Lake I picked up a little auk, which could only have been dead a few hours. It had doubtless been blown in from the sea, and had perished from exhaustion and hunger.

We had scarcely emerged from the swift-flowing river into the smooth waters of the lake, when I made out a caribou crossing a small marsh about half a mile ahead. On approaching closer it seemed, although a large animal, to be hornless, and we thought it was a doe; but whatever it was I determined to shoot it if possible, as we were very meat-hungry, having had nothing but bacon to eat since leaving Millertown.

As we approached nearer to the unsuspicious animal, which never seemed to notice the canoe gliding silently but swiftly towards it, I saw that it had small horns.

It then left the marsh, and walked along the shore of a wooded promontory, and was browsing on some bushes when

I fired at and killed it from the canoe at a distance of not more than fifty yards.

It proved to be a good-sized stag, and judging by its teeth must have been five or six years old, but it carried a miserable little pair of horns. However, I had not shot it for its head but for its meat, and that if not fit for a king was at least very good for a hungry man.

Although it was still early in the day we camped at once alongside the carcase of the slain deer, and were soon feasting on fried steaks with appetites that any primeval savage might have envied.

Whilst walking along the lake-shore in the evening I came across the stump of a large birch tree that had been cut down by beavers apparently about two years previously, but I saw no fresher indications of these animals.

On the morning of October 11th, with a strong wind behind us, we ran down Lloyd's Lake, which is about seven miles long by a mile or so in breadth, very quickly, but after reaching the mouth of the river which runs into it from King George's Lake, we were able to make but very slow progress, for although we worked hard for the rest of the day we were still not much more than two miles from the lake when it began to get dark. We had had to carry the load and then drag the empty canoe over the shallows almost the whole way. We saw fresh bear tracks in the evening.

On the following morning we had the same difficulties to contend with, and found it impossible to get the canoe along without first lightening it, so we carried half the load for about a mile-and-a-half along the river's bank. Then Smart and Geange went back and brought up the canoe with the rest of the load. This took them three hours.

Whilst my men were bringing up the canoe I walked three or four miles up the river. On my way I met a caribou

GEANGE AND SMART AT THE CAMP
ON THE EXPLOITS RIVER.

doe and fawn coming down. At this point there was a space of about five or six yards of ground strewn with boulders and stones between the running water and a high steep bank covered with dense forest.

When I first saw the deer they were about one hundred and fifty yards away, and as the wind was blowing down stream they could not possibly scent me, so I sat down on a rock and waited for them. They came slowly along, picking their way amongst the stones, and every now and again halting to feed on the grass or the leaves of bushes growing on the bank. I sat in full view, about midway between the bank and the water, holding my rifle across my knees, and remained absolutely motionless.

The doe never noticed me at all, and I am sure never for one moment imagined that I was not part of the stone on which I was sitting. She passed slowly between me and the bank, and at one time was certainly not four feet away from me. The fawn walked right on to me, and when its nose was almost touching my knees I think must have smelt me, as it stopped and stood looking into my face with its nostrils twitching. I remained perfectly still and it then turned aside, and walking past me rejoined its mother, without, however, seeming to have taken alarm.

Directly they were past me these caribou got my wind, but even then they did not run, but just walked on till they were out of sight, continually stopping and sniffing the wind, and holding their absurd little tails cocked up.

During the afternoon, in spite of our utmost efforts, we only advanced about a mile up the river, which was very swift, shallow, and full of rocks and boulders.

On October 13th I came to the conclusion that at our present rate of progress it would take at least ten days to reach King George's Lake with the canoe, and so determined to leave it and proceed on foot, just taking a very light cotton sheet, twelve feet by eight feet, and only weighing eight pounds, to protect us from the weather at nights, and our blankets, and enough tea, sugar, and flour to last us ten days or a fortnight, if we always had plenty of meat.

We stowed all the provisions we left behind in bags, which we suspended from the branches of trees with our towing rope, so that no prowling bear could get at them.

During our first day's walk along the river we saw several caribou but no big stag. These caribou were all curiously tame. Two of them allowed us to walk along one side of the river, whilst they kept pace with us on the other, and less than one hundred yards away from us, for more than a mile, when they at last turned into the forest. As the wind was blowing down stream they did not scent us, and I imagine they had never before seen human beings.

In the afternoon we reached the entrance to a canyon, where the river is confined to a narrow channel running between rocky bluffs. We experienced a great deal of trouble following the river along this part of its course, hampered as we were with our packs, and also found it very difficult to reach a place where it was possible to camp. Finally we made a bad camp just at dark. Late in the evening we passed a young caribou stag.

On the following day we had a good deal of light rain, and this was the beginning of a spell of bad weather, which lasted with infrequent intermissions for over a fortnight. During this time we seldom had any heavy rain, but light showers were continually falling. Our clothes were nearly always more or less soaked, but less from the rain than by the drip from the trees and bushes. Our blankets, too, often got rather wet at nights, as a sudden change of wind would sometimes cause the rain to beat in under our shelter.

During this spell of bad weather the wind changed to every point of the compass, but no matter from what quarter it came it always brought rain. However, in Newfoundland one can always find an abundance of dry wood, and build up big fires, and so no matter how wet we got during the day, we always dried everything in the evening, and turned in warm and comfortable.

On the afternoon of October 16th we reached King George the Fourth's Lake, after a hard scramble along the rocky bank of the river almost all the way from where we had left the canoe.

We had seen caribou every day whilst travelling, but no big stags. I had been obliged to shoot a young stag, however, for meat. This animal heard us climbing over some rocks, and at once came charging out of the forest on the other side of the river, grunting repeatedly. No doubt he thought the noise he had heard had been made by a caribou doe or a rival stag.

He was not satisfied when he saw three men with packs on their backs on the further side of the river, but at once plunged into the swift-flowing stream, and came half wading, half swimming towards us. When half way across the river he got our wind, and after standing sniffing the breeze for a considerable time turned back. As his head was not good enough to keep as a trophy, I should have let him go, but my men thought it would be advisable to kill him, and take some of the meat on with us, caching the remainder for use on our return journey.

I spent some days hunting over the bogs and "barrens" lying between the point where the Exploits River flows out of King George's Lake, and a line of hills which is part of a range extending to the north-eastern end of Lloyd's Lake. This range has a general elevation of about two thousand feet, and was known in former days to the Indians by the name of

AN UNNAMED LAKE TO THE EAST OF
KING GEORGE THE FOURTH'S LAKE.

"Annieopsquatsch" There are no Indians there now, but when Mr. Howley surveyed this part of the country he retained the ancient name for this range of hills.

In spite of the wretched weather I saw a good many caribou near King George's Lake. They were all over the open grassy bogs in herds of from eight or ten to over twenty, a big old master stag with each herd. There can be no doubt, I think, that the caribou in this district never migrate to the north across the railway line.

All along the river from Lloyd's Lake we had seen numbers of small spruce trees broken to pieces in the early autumn by stags when clearing their horns of velvet, which is a certain proof that they had passed the summer in the vicinity. All the deer, too, that we saw in this neighbourhood were quiescent, and not travelling. But although I saw a number of big heavy old stags, I did not find a single one with a really good head.

On the evening of the day on which we reached King George's Lake, we saw a herd of about twenty caribou, most of which were lying down, on an open piece of ground beyond the river. I was unable, however, to make out with my glasses, whether or no there was a big stag with them, and as it was already late I did not go after them.

The following day broke in mist and showers of cold sleety rain, but as we wanted meat Geange and I crossed the river soon after breakfast and went up over the broken ground where we had seen the caribou feeding on the preceding evening. Between the river and this open ground we had to pass through a belt of brushwood, and got almost wet through to the skin by the drip from the trees. As we trudged on through the boggy ground, into which we sank ankle-deep at every step, the weather became simply awful. Shower after shower of sleety rain, driven by a hurricane of wind, constantly obscured the desolation of the surrounding landscape, but as we were

GOOD CARIBOU GROUND EAST OF KING
GEORGE TEH FOURTH'S LAKE.

already pretty well wet through we determined to make a good round before returning to camp.

After we had been walking slowly across the wind for a couple of hours—you cannot go very fast through a Newfoundland bog—we came upon a single caribou—a young stag or a doe with horns. We passed this animal and presently saw several more upon the sky-line to leeward.

Leaving my companion behind, I approached these to within three hundred yards behind a few small bushes, and saw that there was a big stag with them, but the wind-driven sleet was beating into my face and I could not use my binoculars nor make out his horns at all well with my eyes, but they seemed to me to be fairly long. He had about twenty does with him, so I thought that he must be a pretty good one that had driven off a lot of weaker stags. Between the little bush from which I was watching and the caribou there was nothing but open level grassy marsh without any kind of cover.

As I was debating what to do, a single doe or a young stag—it had small horns—came across the marsh from behind me, evidently intending to join the herd. As it passed me at a distance of two hundred or three hundred yards, it got my wind, and instead of turning back again, as I had hoped it would do, it ran on and joined the herd, and at once communicated its fears and suspicions to all its members. Up till now most of these had been lying down, but they at once all got up, and the whole herd then commenced to walk away from me, so I left my screen and followed them across the open ground, walking in a crouching attitude.

They presently saw me, but could not make me out in the mist and rain, and I approached without any cover whatever to within two hundred yards of them, before they commenced to run, not straight away, but circling round, evidently with the intention of getting my wind.

As soon as I could get a clear shot at the stag, I fired with the two hundred yards' sight up, and heard the bullet tell. He only ran about one hundred yards and then fell dead. My bullet had struck him just behind the shoulder and gone right through him a little low down, but it must have pierced his heart.

As I was walking up to him another small herd of caribou accompanied by a big old stag came trotting into view, and presently passed within two hundred yards of me. The stag was a big old fellow, and I think I ought to have shot him, as I might very easily have done, as his horns, though not very long, were finely palmated on the brow and bez tines, but as his head was certainly not as good as some I had got in previous years, and as I had already slain one fine animal, I let him go.

The stag I had killed was a big one, but he was very much run down and stank most offensively, the meat being almost uneatable. His horns, too, though well-shaped, were disappointing, being not nearly as heavy as they had appeared through the rain. We got back to camp early in the afternoon with the head and some very poor meat, and spent the rest of the day drying our clothes before a big fire.

The wet stormy weather continued without intermission for nearly four days, and after a respite of only a few hours, came on again worse than ever.

In spite of the rain I went out with Geange every day. We got wet through regularly—more from the drip off the trees and bushes than from the rain itself, which was never heavy—but were always able to dry our clothes on returning to camp before the roaring fire which Smart had waiting for us.

On October 18th we went into some high "barrens" to the north-west of the lake hut saw no caribou at all, although the whole country was covered with their tracks. I think they had all left the open ground and taken shelter from the wind-driven sleet storms in the surrounding forests, where the spruce trees grow so thickly together that it would be almost impossible to get within sight of any animal that had ears to hear.

On the following day we crossed the river and hunted through the country in which I had shot the stag two days before. I was determined to shoot the first caribou doe that I came across, as the meat of the stag last shot was really unfit for human food. As luck would have it, we came on a single doe within a mile of camp. I had no difficulty in getting close up to and despatching this animal, which was in fair condition, though not at all fat. After cleaning the carcase we left it and went on to look for a stag with a good head.

The bogs were now wetter than ever, and as we plodded on through the fine rain we were constantly sinking up to our knees in the soft spongy ground. The whole world seemed half drowned, and I believe that if Noah could have come to life again at this particular time and place and remembered his former experiences upon earth, he would at once have commenced to build another ark.

About midday we came on a stag with five does, but it did not seem to be a very large animal, and its horns were small and light. We passed these caribou below the wind so as not to disturb them, and about an hour later sighted another herd, several of which were lying down just on the edge of a patch of forest. Getting a little nearer I soon saw there was a stag with them, which I hoped might be the possessor of a fine head. These caribou were in an excellent position for a stalk, as the wind was blowing across the open marsh into the piece of forest on the edge of which they were.

Under the shelter of the trees and taking care not to make the slightest noise, I approached to within fifty yards of the stag, and studied his head closely. But though he was a fine

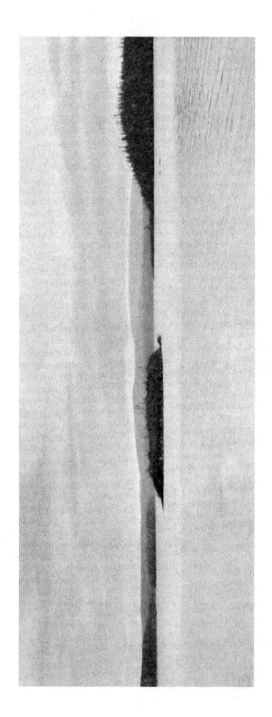

LAKE TO THE NORTH-WEST OF THE SOUTH-WEST END OF LLOYD'S LAKE.

large animal, and his brow and bez tines were fairly well developed, the tops of his horns were very poor, which is a common fault in the heads of caribou stags in Newfoundland. I held his life in my hand and the bad development of the tops of his horns was the only thing that saved it. As it was I crept back again without disturbing him, and left him, all unconscious of my inspection, in charge of the twelve does which formed his harem.

After this we did not travel much further as we were very wet and uncomfortable, and the weather showed no signs of clearing up. On our way home we passed the carcase of the doe I had shot in the morning, and cutting off the two hindquarters carried them to camp.

On the two days on which Geange and I had hunted to the south-east of our camp we had seen some very likely-looking country for caribou stretching away for miles towards the mountain range with the curious Indian name which I have mentioned above.

I determined, therefore, after a consultation with my companions on the evening of October the 19th, to leave our camp on the shore of King George's Lake on the following morning, and march through this country to the foot of the mountains, and from there back to where we had left our canoe and store of provisions on the river.

Although we had now but little to carry in the way of provisions, except a few pounds of flour and a little tea and sugar, yet the wet tarpaulin, together with cooking utensils, the men's blankets, a haunch of venison, and the caribou head and scalp, which I had preserved, made up two good loads for the men, whilst I carried my own blankets, spare clothing and rifle.

When day broke on the morning of October 20th the rain had stopped but the sky looked dark and lowering. A strong wind was blowing from the south-west, before which showers of sleety rain were frequently driven almost horizontally across the waterlogged country. Early in the afternoon, however, it cleared up a little, and we once more saw some blue sky and caught a glimpse of the sun.

In the course of the morning we saw several small bands of caribou which, however, all got our wind, as it was blowing from behind us. Soon after midday we espied a large herd away to our right in the middle of an open marsh. We could see there was a big stag with them, but as it was just then raining I could not tell very well what his horns were like, though I could see with my glasses that he had got horns. As it was about time for a rest and a cup of tea, I told my men to make a fire in a small patch of timber just in front of us, whilst I went to look at the stag.

As I had got the wind right, and as there was not a stick of cover between me and the caribou, I simply walked straight towards them across the bog. They did not appear to notice me until I was within three hundred yards of them; then they all stood looking at me until I had approached well within shot.

The horns of the stag looked to me very fine, and I was quite near enough to take a shot at him, but the cold, sleety rain was beating straight into my eyes in such a way that I found it impossible to do so. Then an old doe started off at a trot, all the rest of the herd following, and the stag bringing up the rear. They only ran about one hundred yards, then wheeling round again stood looking at me for a few moments, and then, with noses outstretched, came trotting back towards me.

I imagine that these caribou had never seen a human being before, and, not knowing what I was, wanted to have a closer view and get my wind. They came and stood within one hundred yards of me, and the old stag looked a grand beast, with his great white neck and broadly palmated horns, but the sleet was cutting into my eyes and half blinding me, and I found it quite impossible to get a sight on him.

Not knowing what to make of me the caribou soon trotted off again for a short distance, and then, breaking into a gallop, commenced to circle round to get my wind. This enabled me very soon to turn my left cheek to the wind and rain, and get my right eye into shelter. Hastily drying it with the corner of my coat, I was once more able to look along my rifle barrel and see the sights plainly.

The caribou just then all halted, and the old stag swinging round stood facing me. I took a steady shot at him from a sitting position with the two hundred yards' sight, and as he turned again I thought I heard the bullet strike. He did not run one hundred yards before falling over, and when I came up to him he was quite dead. My bullet had struck him in the middle of the chest and must have passed through his heart. This stag carried a pretty symmetrical head of thirty-six points, and though not large it was the best I came across during the trip.

On hearing the shot my men came up, and I soon cut the stag's head off, and after having had a cup of tea and something to eat, I skinned it, and Smart then cut all the meat off the skull, which he tied on the top of his pack.

Early in the afternoon we came to a splendid old stag lying fast asleep all by himself. I crept close up to him, but his horns though heavy were very uneven and altogether not at all handsome, so I left him lying asleep.

After this we had some very tiring walking through very wet marshes alternating with belts of gnarled and twisted pine scrub not more than three or four feet in height but growing so thickly matted together that it was only just possible to force one's way through it with a pack on one's back. This stunted growth of pine trees is only met with on the high "barrens" of Newfoundland, and then only in comparatively narrow belts, but getting through even a few hundred yards of it tires one out.

Late in the afternoon we approached a beautiful lake about three miles long by two in breadth, lying just under the mountain range towards which we had been directing our course. I ascertained afterwards from Mr. Howley that he did not know of the existence of this little lake, so it is quite possible that my two companions and myself were the only white men who had ever visited it.

The ease with which one can discover new lakes in Newfoundland is one of the delights of travel in that country. Much of the interior of the island is yet unmapped, and as the whole country is full of "ponds" (as the lakes of all sizes are locally called) anyone who is enterprising enough to go off the beaten track after caribou will at once become an explorer in a small way.

As we approached the lake we saw six herds of caribou feeding on an open grassy plain which lay just below us along its shore. There were from ten to twenty-five animals in each herd, two of which were within a few hundred yards of us, and the furthest not more than a mile away. With my glasses I could make out that there was one big stag with each herd, and the two nearest which I could see clearly with the naked eye, both looked fairly good ones. As, however, both my men were carrying a caribou head on the top of their packs I had determined not to shoot another stag until I had got these two to the point on the river where we had left the canoe.

It was late that evening before we got our camp pitched on a small hillock covered with pine and birch trees, close to the lake-shore, and by that time the sky had once more clouded over, although the two hours before sunset had been quite bright and fine.

During the night rain again commenced to fall and the

weather became very rough, nor did it cease to rain, except for short intervals, until the morning of October 22nd, when it commenced to snow. Before turning in, Smart converted the last of our flour into flat cakes, baked in the frying-pan, and they were just about enough to last us until we reached our store on the river, if we did not delay very long in getting there. Besides the bread and a little tea we still had meat enough for a few more meals.

Saturday, October 21st, was about as bad a day for travelling as one could well imagine, all the beauties of the landscape being obscured by showers of sleety rain. Had we had more food I think we would have lain over a day under the shelter of our tarpaulin, hoping for better things on the morrow, but as it was we had to get on, so we made our way down through the soaking woods to the river, which we reached at about midday, just in the middle of the narrow rocky canyon.

For the last week we had been getting wet regularly every day, but there are degrees of wetness, and we were so thoroughly soaked when we finally waded waist-deep through the river, that I believe we were just as wet through above the water as below it.

We followed the course of the river through the canyon with considerable difficulty, as it is very hard work clambering up and down steep places with a pack on one's back. We finally camped within a few miles of where we had left the canoe, and sat up till late drying our things by a roaring fire. We had kept our blankets dry in waterproof canvas bags.

It rained at intervals during the night, and when we woke up at daylight it was snowing. Light snowstorms continued to fall all day, but in the afternoon the weather improved, and there were intervals when the sun shone out. A walk of two and a half hours down the river after breakfast brought us to the camp where we had left the canoe, and here we found everything as we had left it, untouched by bears or other animals.

On the following morning (October 23rd), we started on an excursion into the country to the north of our camp, expecting to be able to reach open country within a short distance of the river. After making our way for a couple of hours through thick forest we came upon a large lake, several miles in length, and not marked, I think, on the most recent maps of Newfoundland.

We were just approaching the lake-shore when, turning my head, I saw a large caribou stag standing on the water's edge, about two hundred yards away.

Hastily slipping the pack from my back I got my rifle out of its case, loaded it, and sitting down, just got a shot, with the two hundred yards' sight up, as he was starting to run.

Thick scrubby bush grew close down to the edge of the lake, and into this he immediately disappeared. My men thought I had missed, but, although the stag was moving when I fired, I felt sure I had had the sight fairly on him when I pulled the trigger, so I ran round the water's edge as hard as I could to the place where he had disappeared from view, and almost immediately after entering the bush saw him standing with his head down, badly wounded, and killed him with another bullet.

He was a fine specimen of a Newfoundland caribou, standing fifty-two and a half inches at the shoulder, and in fine coat, so as it was so near our camp on the river I preserved his skin entire, and getting it home in good condition, was finally able to add it to the zoological collection in the Natural History Museum, at South Kensington.

After we had pitched camp, and whilst I was busy cleaning the skin of the stag just shot, herd after herd of caribou passed the end of the lake in full view from where we were sitting. These herds were all small, consisting of from three or four to ten animals. They were all following the same trail, and were evidently migrating from the north-east to the south-west. Although they kept stopping to feed they travelled fast, often trotting as if alarmed.

The behaviour of these migrating caribou—many more of which I saw a little later on—was altogether in very marked contrast to that of their near neighbours to the south of the river, near King George's Lake, which we had always found either lying down or feeding quietly on one spot.

Although we saw several caribou stags in the course of the afternoon, none of them carried very good horns, so I let them all pass unmolested.

On the following day the weather was fairly fine except for occasional showers of sleet and snow. In the morning we climbed some trees on the top of a high wooded ridge, but could see no sign of open ground, nothing but dense forest as far as the eye could reach. I resolved, therefore, to carry the caribou skin and head back to our camp on the river in the afternoon, and then return to the little lake where we had seen the six herds of caribou feeding at one time, in the hope of being able to find a stag with a good head amongst them.

This trip, however, met with no success, for the weather once more turned so bad that all the caribou left the open ground and took shelter in the woods, which were so thick that we could never see them there before they heard us. Whilst making our way up the river on the first day, and when still close to camp, we met a stag with small but very pretty horns, which I shot. His teeth showed that he was quite an old animal. We cut off his head and haunches and hung them in a tree to await our return.

During a three days' round, travelling, I should think, something like twenty miles a day, we did not meet with any good stags, though we saw a certain number of caribou every day.

On the evening of October 27th we got back once more to our camp on the river. During the night the weather changed completely, the sky became bright and clear, and it froze hard.

On the following morning we packed up, put our canoe once more in the water, and started down stream for Lloyd's Lake, which we reached very easily and quickly, as, after all the rain, the water was very much higher than when we came up the river.

Reaching the top end of the lake before four o'clock, and finding the wind favourable, we improvised a sail with our light tarpaulin, and running before a strong breeze, reached an old lumbering camp about a mile and a half from the north-eastern end of the lake just as it was getting dark. We saw several caribou on the shore of Lloyd's Lake in the evening, amongst them a big stag.

The following day being Sunday, and the morning being very rainy, we remained at the lumber camp, resting, and drying my skins by the heat of an old stove, to which Smart, with great ingenuity, had fitted several badly damaged pieces of piping, and at last got into good working order. In the evening the weather again cleared up, and I watched several caribou swim across the lake a little below the lumbering camp. They might very easily have walked round the shore of the lake and crossed the river at the end of it, which was less than one hundred yards in breadth, but they plunged into the water just where they struck it without any hesitation, and swam right across (a distance of over a mile) at marvellous speed.

On Monday, October 30th, three caribou, a young stag, a doe, and a last year's fawn, jumped into the water and swam close past our canoe almost immediately we left the old lumber camp. We stopped paddling as soon as they entered the lake, and as they had not got our wind they did not take alarm at the sight of the canoe, but swam past within a hundred yards of us. They were then swimming very fast, but after they had got a little further out into the lake they scented us, and after stopping for a moment to look round, they went off at a greatly increased rate of speed. They very soon landed on the further shore, along which, after first having shaken themselves like dogs, they trotted for some distance before turning into the forest.

No other animal that I have ever seen swimming keeps so much of its body above the water as a caribou. About a third of the whole length of the body is always above the surface, and the little saucy-looking tail, the underpart of which is snowy-white, is always carried cocked straight in the air. The buoyancy of the caribou when swimming is no doubt due to the peculiarity of its coat, every hair of which is hollow and filled with air, so that these animals may be said to be clothed in a lifebelt.

After leaving Lloyd's Lake we proceeded down the Exploits River (more commonly known as Lloyd's River) to the foot of a mountain known as Mount Ramsay, and camped at the mouth of a creek, which, judging by the amount of water it brought down, my men said must have its source in a good-sized lake. The next morning, with packs on our backs, we followed the course of the creek to the shoulder of Mount Ramsay and, putting down our loads, climbed nearly to the top of the mountain, in order to get a view over the surrounding country. To our right we could see a good-sized lake in which no doubt the creek whose course we had been following took its rise. To the north-west lay a great expanse of open ground, the nearest part of which was not more than a couple of miles distant, though it took us some time to get through the intervening forest, which was very dense.

ON THE WAY DOWN THE EXPLOITS RIVER.

We pitched our camp about midday in a thick patch of forest just on the edge of some high "barrens" from which a splendid view of the country on ahead was obtainable. A chain of small lake; lay just below us, and beyond these a great stretch of open grassy marshes. Over these marshes I at once saw two lots of caribou passing, all of them travelling rapidly towards the south-west.

After having had something to eat, I made a round in the afternoon past the nearest lake and on to the open ground beyond. I found the whole country covered with caribou paths, all leading from the north-east to the south-west, and judging by the way in which these trails were tracked up I have no hesitation in saying that several hundreds of caribou must have passed through these marshes alone during the previous month. During the afternoon we saw three big stags, one with a herd of does; and the other two travelling by themselves, but none of them had good heads, so I left them alone.

On the morning of November 1st I took both Smart and Geange with me on to the marshes beyond the lakes, as I wanted to bring back a good supply of meat to camp as well as a fine head if I could see a good stag.

We soon spied a herd of eight caribou coming across the marsh, so leaving my companions in a hollow through which a small stream ran into one of the chain of lakes, I cut across in front of them to see if there was a good stag with them.

I soon saw that the only male amongst them was not worth shooting, so let them all pass, and was then returning to where I had left Smart and Geange, when I saw another herd coming across the open ground and making straight for where my men were standing, though as they were in the bed of the creek the caribou were still invisible to them.

The herd numbered ten animals, one of which I could see through my glasses was a good-sized stag. They came rapidly across the marsh, sometimes trotting, at others halting to eat a little moss or grass. It was presently evident that they were making exactly for the spot where my men were sitting close to a caribou trail which led across the creek, so I told them to go a little higher up and hide amongst some bushes. Meanwhile, I took up a position on the open marsh, about fifty yards from the creek.

Here I sat perfectly still though in full view—for I had learnt that the caribou in Newfoundland never seem to notice a human being as long as he stands quite still—and watched the herd coming on, the wind blowing across the marsh in such a way that they could not scent me without passing behind me. A doe with a pretty pair of horns was leading, the stag bringing up the rear of the herd, but when he had come up to within one hundred yards of me I saw that he was not worth shooting.

By this time the leading doe was on the point of crossing the creek, but she never did so, for when within a few yards of it, she stopped dead, and with her head raised stood stock-still sniffing the air. She evidently smelt the taint left on the ground some ten yards away where Geange and Smart had been sitting and would not advance a step farther.

After standing perfectly still for several minutes, during which time all the other members of the herd (except the stag which had never ceased grazing) stood looking at her, the suspicious animal at last turned round and walked slowly back the way she had come, always keeping her head raised and her little tail cocked up. Presently they all worked round on to their former course and got behind me. They then got my wind and scurried off towards the south-west, and never stopped again as long as they were in sight.

We did not see any more caribou until the afternoon, when a large band came in sight. They were travelling very rapidly, making for the chain of lakes which I thought they intended to cross, but reaching the shore of one of them they followed its course towards where we were standing. Leaving my companions I now made for the lake, and presently took up a position amongst some small pine scrub within one hundred yards of the water, or rather ice, for during the two previous nights we had had sharp frosts, and the small upland lakes were now all covered with a sheet of ice.

Some two hundred yards in advance of the herd three fine old stags came walking rapidly along, one behind the other. They were all large full-grown animals, with great white shaggy necks, but only one had a well-developed pair of horns; those of the other two, although they were broadly palmated on the lower tines, being badly grown on the tops.

I may here say that 1905 was a bad year for caribou heads in Newfoundland, and I believe that no really fine antlers were obtained in any part of the island during that season. This defective horn growth I attribute to the severity of the previous winter and the deep snow which covered the country in the spring, a state of things which kept the stags half-starved and therefore weak at the time their horns were growing.

When the largest of these three stags was exactly opposite to me, and close to the edge of the water, I fired at and hit him exactly in the middle of the shoulder. My bullet, as I found out afterwards, went right through him, breaking both shoulders, but it must have missed his heart, as it did not kill him.

Directly I fired, dropping the big stag on the spot, his two companions came trotting past me on the one side, whilst the herd came close up to where I was sitting. I counted them and found they numbered twenty-six altogether, two of them being young stags, and all the rest does and last year's fawns; so that with the three big stags the herd had consisted of twenty-nine animals altogether.

On walking up to examine my prize, which I thought

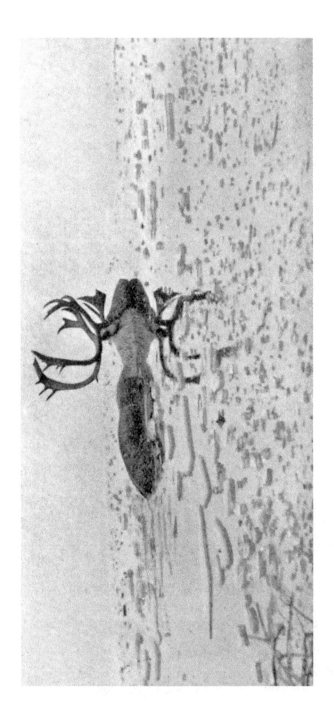

WOUNDED CARIBOU BREAKING THROUGH
THE ICE ON A SMALL LAKE.

was dead, he gave a tremendous heave with his hind legs, which were uninjured, and threw himself off the steep bank, on the edge of which he had been lying, on to the ice below, through which he crashed, and then, with a series of plunges, broke his way some twenty yards out into the lake. I then killed him with a bullet through the lungs, and Smart got out to the carcase with the help of poles laid over the ice, and brought it in to shore. This caribou carried a fairly good head but not at all a remarkable one.

Although through the kindness of the authorities in St. John's, I had been granted a special permit to kill as many caribou as I might require to keep myself in fresh meat on my journey to and from King George's Lake—for one cannot carry much meat in addition to a heavy pack—I determined now to stay my hand, for I had seen so many big stags with poor heads, that I did not think it very likely I would get a really good one by hunting for a few days longer, and I did not want to kill any more with only moderate heads.

So on November 2nd we returned to our camp on the river, and the same afternoon paddled a few miles down stream. On the following day we reached the head of Red Indian Lake before midday. There had been a sharp frost the night before, followed by one of the most beautiful days imaginable. After all the wretched rainy weather we had had ever since leaving Red Indian Lake more than three weeks previously how we did appreciate that first really bright warm sunny day!

Running down the lake before a favouring breeze we made at least twenty miles before camping on an island some time after dark. Except when running across deep bays we always kept fairly near the northern shore of the lake in case of accidents.

We saw two herds of caribou emerge from the forest surrounding the lake, trot a short distance along the beach, and then plunge without the slightest hesitation into the water, and start on their five-mile swim to the other side.

On the following day the wind was against us, but by dint of six hours' hard paddling we reached Millertown at three o'clock in the afternoon, having run the whole length of Red Indian Lake (forty miles) in exactly twelve hours.

We found Millertown deserted, but in the evening four men turned up, who were taking care of the houses, and who had been away hunting. We had, however, already installed ourselves, and lighted the stove in a comfortable cabin into which Smart had managed to effect an entrance, and here we spent a comfortable night. As the train had now ceased running from Millertown to the main line, eighteen miles distant, the only way to get there with my camp outfit and heads was by trolley, leaving my canoe to be brought out later on.

The next day was a Sunday (November 5th), and about as coarse a day as I had ever known—snowing, sleeting and raining all day long without a moment's cessation. We had to push the trolley for the first nine miles, as it would not run on the frozen rails, but after midday we were able to pump it along, and in the evening we reached Millertown Junction on the main line from Port-aux-Basques to St. John's, wet to the very skin and chilled to the bone.

On the following day in the best of health after my little outing I once more reached St. John's, where I was most kindly received and hospitably entertained by my old friend Judge D. W. Prowse and his wife, at their charming residence on the outskirts of the town.

With my return to St. John's my third trip after caribou in the bogs, forests and "barrens" of the interior of Newfoundland came to an end.

CHAPTER VIII.

HUNTING ON THE
SOUTH FORK OF THE
MACMILLAN RIVER.

EARLY IN 1906 I again grew restless, and as a short trip to
Bosnia, in April of that year, in search of nests and eggs of the
nutcracker, did but little to still the voices of the wilderness
that were for ever whispering to me of far-away game-haunted
mountains and forests, I started once more for the Macmillan
River in the Yukon Territory of North-western Canada on
July 12th, and reached Skagway, Alaska, on August 1st.

Four days later, on the evening of Sunday, August 5th,
I started from Whitehorse on my long canoe journey to the
south fork of the Macmillan River. I might have travelled the
three hundred miles down the Yukon from Whitehorse to
Selkirk by steamer, and saved a couple of days by so doing; but
this would have cost me at least one hundred dollars; and as
I had a good twenty-foot canoe, to carry me down the swift-
flowing river, and the weather was fine, I had no hesitation in
commencing my canoe journey from Whitehorse.

For the loan of the canoe which I used on this trip, I was
indebted to the great kindness of Mr. H. Wheeler, the traffic

SALMON DRYING AT SELKIRK.
Photograph by CARL RUNGIUS.

manager of the White Pass and Yukon Railway, who did everything possible to assist me.

Of the two men who accompanied me, the one, Charles Coghlan, had been with Mr. Sheldon and myself up the north fork of the Macmillan two years previously, and I, therefore, knew him well. He is not only a splendid specimen of a man physically, almost literally as strong as a bull, but he is also one of the best tempered and most good natured fellows I have ever met, never tiring of hard work or losing his cheerful good spirits.

My other man, Rhoderick Thomas, I knew well by reputation, although I had never met him before this trip. He had accompanied my old friend, Mr. J. B. Tyrrell, on his most arduous journeys through the barren grounds of Northern Canada and along the shores of the Arctic sea to Fort Churchill, and had been one of his most trusted canoemen. Rhoderick Thomas (always called "Tommy" in the Yukon) I found well deserved the good character I had heard given to him. He is an excellent canoeman, woodsman, and packer, and withal a most cheery good tempered willing man. I could not very well have had two better men with me than Coghlan and Thomas.

We had very fine weather for our trip down the Yukon to Selkirk, and after we had got through Lake Lebarge, which is thirty-five miles long, we often travelled at the rate of ten miles an hour, using two paddles and a pair of sculls, and aided by the strong current. In two days we did one hundred and ninety-six miles from Lake Lebarge to the now abandoned police station of Minto, going down the Five Finger rapids, and several other stretches of swift water, without any difficulty.

On the morning of August 9th we reached Selkirk. So far we had met with but little of interest. A porcupine moving leisurely along the water's edge early one morning was the only animal we had seen, and the bird-life had been very limited, both in species and individuals.

LANSING CREEK INDIANS, NORTH
FORK, STEWART RIVER.
Photograph by D.O. CAMERON.

Whilst crossing Lake Lebarge we saw an osprey plunge into the lake, and rise from the water carrying a good-sized fish in its claws. Sandpipers (*Actitis macularia*) were numerous all along the river, and the handsome American kingfisher (*Ceryle alcyon*) was not uncommon. A few sand martins still lingered near the mud cliffs in which they had nested, and numbers of nightjars (*Chordeiles virginianus*) were to be seen hawking for flies every evening during the long drawn-out twilight of this subarctic land. These, with a few ducks and mergansers, and an odd hawk, raven or buzzard, were almost the only birds I remember to have seen.

At the mouth of the Little Salmon River, and at several other places, we passed small encampments of Indians, all engaged in catching and drying salmon. These Yukon Indians are almost all short of stature, but strongly built. Their hair is very coarse and black, and their whole appearance suggests a closer relationship to the inhabitants of North-east Asia than to the typical North American Indians of the countries to the east of the Rocky Mountains.

Many of the Indians I saw in the Yukon and on the Pacific coast of British Columbia looked to me strangely like Japanese, and I cannot help thinking that whether or no the ancestors of all the aboriginal inhabitants of North and South America came to those continents from Asia by way of Behring Straits, the forefathers of the Indians of Alaska and the North Pacific coast must certainly have done so in comparatively recent times.

After a slight delay in Selkirk we crossed the Yukon and entered the mouth of the Pelly, reaching the farm, which is being worked by two French Canadians, about three miles up the river, early in the afternoon.

These men have cleared about fifty acres of land along the bank of the river of all trees and bush; and grow good crops of potatoes and oats in the light loamy soil. The oats are cut before they are fully ripe, and used as-green forage for horses. The potatoes mature and ripen much. More quickly in this northern country than in more southerly latitudes, as they get so much more sunlight whilst they are growing.

We heard from one of the farmers that a party of Selkirk Indians, who had lately been catching salmon a couple of miles further up the river, had quite recently killed four moose near their camp, and that during the spring and summer a single Indian belonging to another tribe had killed sixteen of these animals—of course, most of them cows and calves—in the country between the lower Peily and the Stewart River.

Fortunately for the game of Alaska and the Yukon territory Indians are not very numerous in those countries, and are supposed to be decreasing in numbers, for they are certainly very destructive.

Formerly, the only hunters in the country were Indians armed with spears and bows and arrows, and the toll these primitive savages levied on the game was probably not very heavy; but the Indian hunter of to-day is armed with a Winchester repeating rifle of the latest pattern, and according to several trappers, to whom I talked on the subject, he kills a great deal more game than is generally supposed, never missing an opportunity of killing an animal, whether he wants it or not.

Besides the half-civilised Indians, there are the white trappers, the prospectors and the miners, all of whom must kill game or get it killed for them, or go without fresh meat. The trappers have but little time for big game hunting, and as a rule only kill a very limited number of moose and caribou. The prospectors, too, wander about killing a head of game here and there, but are not regular hunters, and often travel long distances without seeing game or tasting meat.

Personally, I regard these two classes of white men as not very destructive to large game, and would place in the same category the few sportsmen, who visit this far-away country in the hope of securing a few good heads, and who do not kill females or young animals except when it is necessary to do so, in order to get meat.

It is undoubtedly the discovery of gold which has caused, and will continue to bring about, a very wholesale destruction of game in Alaska and the Yukon, for miners collect in camps, wherever gold is found, and as they are always ready to pay a good price for fresh meat they give employment to meat-hunters, who are able to make a good deal of money by killing game and selling the meat at the nearest mining town or camp. Such men, of course, kill everything—wild sheep ewes and lambs, moose and caribou cows and calves—and soon deplete large areas of country of game.

During the winter of 1903-04 fifteen hundred caribou were killed by meat-hunters during the autumn migration across the upper waters of the Klondyke River and their frozen carcases brought on sledges for one hundred and eighty miles to Dawson City.

In the autumn of 1904, too, there were men hunting moose near the forks of the Macmillan, the meat of which they intended to carry down to Dawson, on rafts, a distance of four hundred miles. They told me they could get thirty cents a pound for moose meat in Dawson, so that each moose shot would probably be worth to them, on an average from twenty pounds to twenty-five pounds.

In the late autumn of 1904 a large band of caribou on migration southwards crossed the Yukon, a long way below Dawson City, and struck the newly-erected telegraph line leading to the town of Fairbanks, which at that time consisted of a number of log cabins, scattered over a valley in which good gold prospects had only recently been discovered.

Instead of crossing the line of telegraph poles the caribou followed all along it, until they reached the settlement through which they proceeded to pass. The inhabitants turned out en masse, and are said to have killed six hundred of them. One big stag put its head into an open cabin door, and could not withdraw its great wide-spreading horns, and was killed with an axe by a man who was inside the cabin.

With all these agencies at work upon its destruction, no doubt game is being rapidly killed off in certain areas of Alaska and the Yukon territory, but vast stretches of country still remain where no gold has been found. There the game is practically unmolested, and I hope and believe that for ages yet to come, moose, caribou, wild sheep and bears, in certain districts of these vast territories, will continue to find safe retreats, in which they will be but seldom disturbed by either white or Indian hunters.

On the morning of August 10th, the day after we had passed the farm on the lower Pelly, I was walking along the bank of the river, about a mile ahead of the canoe, when I saw something coming down the stream, which I soon made out to be a moose cow, with just its head and ears above water. It was making across the river, but the strong current carried it down so swiftly that it came past me when still in mid-stream.

I fired at it, at a range of something over one hundred yards, and its head immediately dropped and went under water, and I thought I had killed it. But presently it began to flounder about, and its head came up again. Then evidently dazed and half-stunned it came swimming slowly back towards the side of the river where I was standing, and I killed it as it came ashore, with a shot through the lungs.

The first shot, I found, had struck it high up on the left cheek, and had come out just below the right ear, and could only just have missed the brain. The animal proved to be a young cow in very fair condition.

This supply of good fresh meat was most fortunate and unexpected, as I had not hoped to come across anything in the way of game until we had got far up the Macmillan River.

After loading up as much meat as we could carry on our canoe, we proceeded on our way, and slept that night on an island just below two rocks standing in the middle of the river, known as the Gull Rocks, as they form the nesting site of a colony of American herring gulls (*Larus argentatus smithsunianus*). As the current in the Pelly and Macmillan Rivers is far too swift to make headway against by paddling, the only way to get a canoe along is by poling and towing. Only two men are required for this, so I left the management of the canoe entirely to Coghlan and Thomas, both of whom are very experienced men in this kind of work. They took it in turn to pole and tow, and by working very hard for nine or ten hours every day made an average of about eighteen miles, a very good rate of travel, I think, under all the circumstances.

I walked the whole way along the bank and tried to keep a good distance ahead of the canoe in the hope of seeing game before it had been disturbed by the canoe, for poling makes a good deal of noise. Right up to the 27th of August we had almost continuous fine weather, and the sun was often quite oppressively hot. Mosquitoes and midges were a little troublesome in the afternoons and evenings, but not excessively so.

The walking I often found most fatiguing, as, wherever the forest came right down to the bank of the river, there was always a luxuriant undergrowth of wild rose and other bushes, beneath which lay a network of fallen trees, through and over which one could only make one's way very slowly and painfully. Amongst this undergrowth I found both black and red currant bushes growing, but nowhere in great profusion. The

COTTONWOOD TREE (18 inches in
diameter) CUT DOWN BY BEAVERS.

berries on the latter were very fine. Here and there, too, I found wild raspberries.

Bear tracks—nearly all, I think, those of black bears—were plentiful all along the Macmillan, but I never had the luck to see one on the open bars, and amongst the thick undergrowth there was no chance of doing so.

As we approached the forks of the Macmillan signs of the presence of beavers became frequent, and I came across a good many large cottonwood trees which they had lately cut down.

These interesting animals, however, were not nearly so plentiful in 1906 as I had found them in 1904, a great number having been trapped a few months before my last visit by a band of Indians, who had come over to the upper Macmillan from the Little Salmon River. During the very cold weather which occurred in January, 1906—said to have been the coldest ever recorded in the Yukon—this band of Indians had every dog they possessed frozen to death.

Besides the considerable number of beavers trapped by the Indians at this time, forty-three were also caught by two white trappers, so that probably more than one hundred were killed in a few weeks in this district, in which, up to that year, they had lived unmolested for a very long time.

On August 13th we got through the Pelly Canyon without any difficulty, and shortly afterwards met a solitary old prospector floating down the river in a boat that was built a long way up the Pelly, where he had been unsuccessful in finding payable gold. He told us he had not seen a living thing on his long journey down stream until he met us, neither a white man, nor an Indian, nor a moose, nor a bear. He was well off for provisions of all kinds except meat, of which we were able to give him enough to last him to Selkirk.

On August 18th I fired the first shot since killing the moose the day after leaving Selkirk, and bagged a lynx, and on the following day we took our first day's rest since leaving Whitehorse.

On the morning of August 22nd we ate the last of our fresh meat for breakfast, and not long afterwards a moose cow swam across the river about three hundred yards ahead of our canoe, which I would certainly have killed had I been able to do so, in order to secure a further supply of good meat. But the stream was very strong just where we were, and we could not get a yard nearer to the moose, which soon got across the river and landed under some overhanging bushes amongst which I could not see it.

Soon after this we reached the cabin under Plateau Mountain, where Mr. Sheldon and I had spent a couple of days in 1904. We found two trappers, both of them Englishmen, for whom we had brought letters from Selkirk, installed in the comfortable log hut (which one of them had helped to build four years previously). This latter gentleman had then only lately taken his discharge from the North-west Mounted Police force, and had been earning his living by trapping ever since.

His first winter's trapping, he told me, had been very re-munerative, as he and one companion had caught nearly three hundred martens in prime fur, besides a number of lynxes, mink, and other animals. During the second winter, however, they only trapped some thirty martens on the same ground. During both these seasons he had set his traps low down near the river, but he now intended laying out his lines for traps for the coming winter's work high up near the limit of timber growth on the side of the mountain.

Although a trapper is only actually engaged in trapping from October to May, whilst the fur-bearing animals are in prime coat, yet he has plenty of work to occupy his time dur-ing the rest of the year. Soon after the ice breaks up in the early summer, the trappers go down on the top of the flood to sell their pelts at Selkirk or Dawson, and lay in a supply of provisions and other necessaries for the coming year. Then they start once more, either two together or absolutely alone, on their long slow journey against the stream to their far-away trapping grounds on the upper Pelly or Macmillan Rivers.

During the summer and early autumn they are kept busy chopping trails through the forest along which they set their traps, and in building and provisioning small log cabins at various places in which they can take refuge during the bitter cold of the winter's nights.

An energetic trapper will have as much as forty miles of trail, along which his traps are set, to look after, and will try and visit every trap on all his trails at least once a week throughout the winter. During September every trapper tries to shoot his winter's meat, and get it stored in his various cabins.

In this part of America the moose supplies the trapper's wants almost entirely, as this animal can be found along the rivers near the usual trapping grounds, whilst the wild sheep and caribou do not often leave the mountain ranges.

In September moose bulls become exceedingly fat, and their meat is then equal to good beef, and as the nights are by that time already cold, it can be kept quite sweet until the following summer. When trappers have no dogs they do not require to shoot much game, but each dog kept would probably eat as much meat during the long winter as its master.

I learned from our friends at Plateau Mountain that dogs are not only most useful to them as draught animals in the winter, when small light sledges can be pulled almost anywhere over the snow, but, that if properly packed, and the weather is not too hot, they can carry heavier loads in proportion to their weight than any other four-footed animal. Pointing to one of his dogs, a half-bred husky, with very likely a strain of wolf in it, Mr. P——, the ex-North-west Mounted policeman, assured

TRAPPER'S CABIN ON THE MACMILLAN
BELOW PLATEAU MOUNTAIN.
Photograph by W. OSGOOD.

me that it could carry its own weight—sixty pounds—day after day as long as the weather was not hot.

In the course of conversation, Mr. P—— told me that
although he had come across and shot a few grizzly bears, he
had never had any sort of an adventure with one of these animals. He had, however, once been severely bitten in the leg and
laid up for three weeks by a lynx which he had caught in a steel
trap, and which he was endeavouring to kill with a stick.

The day before we reached their cabin our friends the
trappers had shot a fine bull moose, and secured a very welcome supply of fresh meat, as they had seen no game on their
way up the river from Selkirk, and had had to feed their dogs
on rice when they were unable to catch any salmon in the net
they carried with them.

They had seen the moose feeding amongst some willows
on the other side of the river, and only a few hundred yards
from their cabin, and Mr. P—— had crossed over in their
boat and shot it at very close range. They very kindly gave us
a fresh supply of fine fat meat. The horns of this moose, Mr.
P—— informed me, were not at all large, and were still covered with velvet.

We learned here that an American trapper with his wife
and three children were getting ready to pass the winter in
a cabin about eight miles further up the river, and that two
young Englishmen, Messrs. A—— and L——, were working
some gold-bearing ground on Russell Creek, which runs into
the Macmillan River about three miles below the forks.

I had met Mr. A——on Russell Creek in 1904, and, subsequently, with his wife in England; and I knew that both of
them, as well as Mr. and Mrs. L——, had passed the preceding
winter all by themselves in this far away land. I had brought
letters from Selkirk for Mr. and Mrs. A——, and was much
looking forward to renewing my acquaintance with them.

We did not delay very long at the Plateau Mountain cabin, but pushed on again before midday; and in the afternoon reached the cabin where Mr. Hosfall had installed himself with his wife and children.

The whole family with their four large dogs had only just come back from a trip to a range of mountains about ten miles to the south. They had been away from the river for eighteen days and had only seen two young bull moose all the time, one of which Mr. Hosfall had shot.

Mrs. Hosfall, who is very well-known in the Yukon country, is quite a remarkable woman. The daughter of a Scotsman married to an Indian, she has inherited nothing but the best qualities of both races. She can carry a heavy pack or manage a boat or canoe, in any kind of water, with pole or paddle, as well as her husband, and is reported to be his superior in her knowledge of everything appertaining to woodcraft and the trapping of fur-bearing animals. At the same time she is a well-educated, well-informed woman, who can impart her knowledge of the wild creatures she has lived amongst in perfectly pronounced and softly spoken English.

Of the Hosfall's four children—all girls—the eldest was being educated at the mission school at Selkirk. The three that were with their parents were sweetly pretty little creatures, with rosy cheeks and fine dark eyes.

Last year Mrs. Hosfall and her children met with a terrible adventure, which I will relate as it was told me by her husband.

"In the spring of 1905 I went down to Selkirk to get provisions, leaving my wife and children in the cabin, far away up the Pelly River, in which we had all lived during the previous winter. I told my wife that I would try and get back by a certain date towards the end of May and made every effort to do so.

"One evening on my return journey I camped late some distance above the canyon, and was preparing to get under my blankets, when I heard a boat being rowed down the river. I went down to the water's edge to listen, and soon became convinced that it was my own boat, the boat which I had left with my wife, that was approaching, as from the way in which the pins were set, on which the oars turned, a certain clicking noise resulted which there was no mistaking.

"Full of conjectures as to what could have happened, I holloed loudly as the boat came nearer, and was answered by my wife, who soon brought the boat ashore.

"She told me that two nights before, the cabin in some way got alight from the stove, whilst she and the children were asleep, and they had only. just been able to escape with nothing on but their nightdresses. Everything was burnt—cabin, provisions, clothes, and pelts—and my wife and my three poor little children were left standing in the wilderness without food or shelter.

"My boat was still in good order, so my wife put the children into it, and at once started for Selkirk, three hundred miles distant. The river was in flood, as the ice had only just gone out, and rowing and floating alternately on the strong stream day and night, racing against death to the children from starvation and cold, my wife was prepared to attempt the passage of the Pelly Canyon by night—a most terrible risk to run—in order to reach Selkirk as soon as possible, for I was before my time, and she did not expect to meet me on my return journey.

"It was very fortunate she did so, for my poor little children were near death's door, from starvation and exposure to the bitter cold, when I got them ashore."

On the afternoon of Friday, August 24th, we reached the cabin near the mouth of Russell Creek, which had been built three years previously by the trappers John Barr and George Crosby.

IN CAMP, PLATEAU MOUNTAIN.

Finding no one here, and having letters for Mr. and Mrs. Armstrong, I walked up to their camp at the mine-twelve miles of bad trail. Starting from the river soon after four I got there about eight o'clock, just as it was getting dark, and received a very warm welcome from my friends, who, with Mr. and Mrs. Leith, had got through the long severe winter quite comfortably, and enjoyed very good health all the time.

Mr. Armstrong told me that during the winter, moose had collected in great numbers along Russell Creek to browse on the birch and willow trees which grow there in great profusion.

Once he and his wife when out on snow shoes along the trail, had seen from one spot twenty-five moose, scattered around the hillsides singly or in twos and threes. On another occasion towards the end of the year Mr. Armstrong had seen a. eleven moose all together. This band consisted of nine bulls and a cow and a calf. The leading bull, my friend said, was much larger in body than any of the others, and carried an enormous pair of horns.

This giant bull had frequented the valley of Russell Creek all through the winter, and had been seen by the other two members of Mr. Armstrong's party, as well as by John Barr the trapper, but no one had been able to get a fair shot at him.

Directly after breakfast the next morning I started back for the river, which I reached before one o'clock.

Soon after this we resumed our journey, and getting to the forks of the Macmillan early in the afternoon, camped that night some miles up the south fork.

Late on the following day, August 26th, I saw a cow moose running across an open bar some four hundred yards ahead of the canoe near to which I then was. It had no doubt heard the noise made by the iron prong at the end of the pole striking against a rock. It soon reached the river, which was now quite narrow, and plunging in swam across and disappeared in a thick bed of willows. Being now again out of meat I should have shot this moose had I been able to do so, but it gave me no chance.

About this part of the river there were a great many bear tracks, some quite fresh, and I expected every minute to see one of the animals themselves, looking for dead and dying salmon along the bars. However, I never saw a bear, black or brown, during my whole trip.

The salmon which penetrate every summer to the head-waters of all the tributaries of the upper Yukon—a journey of over two thousand miles from the sea—are said never to return, but to die after spawning. I saw some in the water of a sickly yellowish colour, and evidently in the last stage of debility; and found the remains of many dead ones along the water's edge!

I think I was a little too late for bears, most of which had left the river and gone to the hills after berries.

Although we had had a few showers of rain on our way up the Macmillan the weather had been on the whole very fine and the sun often oppressively hot, but on the morning of August 27th the sky became completely overcast and heavy rain set in.

On the afternoon of that day we reached an old cabin, which had been built by a trapper named Riddell some years before. This cabin was not far from the foothills of a fine range of mountains lying between the south fork of the Macmillan and the Pelly River, so I determined to use it as a base, and to carry some provisions and a light camp outfit up nearly to the limit of forest growth. From there I could hunt the bare mountains above in search of caribou.

On the morning of Tuesday, August 28th, with heavy packs on our backs, we started for the mountains; and late in the afternoon when, after an exceedingly tiring climb, we were at length approaching the open downs above the timber-line, we sighted two caribou high up on the hillside above us.

As we had now been some days without fresh meat it was at once decided that I should try and shoot one of them, and that whilst I was doing so, Coghlan and Thomas should push on up the valley we were then following, and look for a good camping-place near its head. They were to go on by short stages, taking it in turns to go back and bring on my pack.

Relieved of this burden I climbed rapidly towards the caribou, which I found to be a doe and a fawn. Just as I was getting near them a very heavy storm of cold rain came on, and I was soon drenched to the skin, The two caribou now came towards me, and presently were within one hundred and fifty yards, but the rain was just then pouring down in such a way that I couldn't well shoot. Suddenly they got my wind and ran. They did not go far; however, before stopping to look round, and, as the rain was then not falling quite so heavily, I got a shot at about two hundred yards, and badly wounded the doe, which I killed with another shot.

I was sorry to have had to kill this animal, but a plentiful supply of meat was an absolute necessity to us, as we were only able to carry a very limited quantity of any other kind of provisions up into the mountains. Meat, therefore, had to be our main stand-by.

The fawn, I think, was quite old enough to graze, and doubtless soon joined others of its kind. I disembowelled the dead caribou as quickly as possible, as the rain was now coming on again, and then cutting off a good load of meat, to which I added the tongue, liver and kidneys, presently rejoined my companions.

It was late that evening before we got our camp pitched and a good fire alight; but before nightfall the rain stopped altogether, and after we had made a good supper we dried our wet clothes before the fire and got under our blankets quite ready for a long night's rest.

HEAD OF CARIBOU SHOT AUGUST 29, 1906.

On the following morning I sent Coghlan and Thomas to bring in the meat of the caribou doe, and went out by myself to look for a stag worth shooting for his head.

Our camp was situated at the bottom of a ravine down which ran a fine clear mountain stream. We were close to the limit of the growth of spruce and birch trees, which were succeeded along the banks of the creek by a few patches of willow scrub, some four or five feet in height.

The sides of the ravine rose steeply on either side to the edge of what I may term upland plateaux, on which there were neither trees nor bushes of any kind. Where, however, the ground was not covered with stones there was abundant feed for caribou in the shape of moss and short grass.

Scattered over these stretches of open caribou-frequented ground, which were divided one from another by deep ravines, were numerous stony ridges, which in many places made the ground easy for stalking.

I should fancy that these gently-rounded or flat-topped mountains were from five to six thousand feet above sea level, and only in one portion of the range we were on could the altitude have reached the neighbourhood of seven thousand feet. Here the character of the ground was bare rock almost devoid of any vegetation whatever.

On leaving camp on the morning of August 29th I first followed the bed of the ravine for perhaps a mile and a half and then climbed to the edge of the plateau to my left.

As soon as I reached the open ground I saw some caribou—a doe and a fawn—about a mile to my left, and four others, which I presently made out with my glasses to be a small stag with two does and a fawn, near the top of the hill to my right.

Presently, when I had walked a couple of miles or so across the open ground, I sighted another small herd, which

I soon saw with my glasses consisted of seven animals, one of which was a stag.

The stag presently walked up to the top of a stony ridge, where he stood out well against the sky-line, and I could then see his horns quite plainly. They seemed to me to be about the length of those of an average full-grown caribou stag in Newfoundland, and I judged the animal that bore them, therefore, to be still young—as the full-grown stags of the mountain ranges of the Yukon carry very long and very massive horns.

I thought, however, that I had better try and get a nearer view, and to do this I had to make a somewhat lengthy stalk in order to approach the herd from below the wind.

I had got within three hundred yards of the deer, when I saw that a single doe had separated herself from her companions and was walking straight towards me, so I sat down on a rock and waited for her to pass. She came steadily on, and presently walked slowly past and within twenty yards of where I sat in full view but perfectly motionless. She never once looked towards me, in fact, she never noticed me.

After she had passed me this doe walked straight on, without ever stopping to feed, until she presently got my wind. She was then quite three hundred yards beyond me, and about six hundred from the small herd she had left. Immediately she scented me she stopped, and facing round stood sniffing the breeze. Finally she trotted off, holding her short tail cocked up in the air, as is the way of all caribou when alarmed.

The herd, amongst which was the young stag, had now fed over a little knoll, up to which I ran, as fast as I could, across the open ground. Then, going down on my hands and knees, I crept forwards towards the top of the rise, and presently saw the upper part of the stag's horns.

I now lay flat down, and creeping noiselessly a few yards further; raised my head very slowly until I could see all six caribou, which were feeding, quite unconscious of danger, not thirty yards away from me. The stag; I now saw, was a comparatively young animal, with horns of about three feet in length, and still in the velvet.

I lay watching these caribou until they had fed away to a distance of fifty or sixty yards from me. Then, not caring whether they saw me or not, I sat up, and almost immediately a doe and a fawn came feeding back towards me, and were soon followed by the rest. I remained absolutely motionless, but in full view, and the caribou never seemed to notice me at all.

The doe and fawn passed me first, certainly within eight yards, and I noticed that the former had small horns covered with velvet, and that she was still in her summer coat-very dark brown all over, with no white on the neck. The other three does were a little further away.

The stag came last, and I am not exaggerating by an inch, when I say that he came to within four yards of me, without showing the slightest sign that he distinguished me in any way from the rest of the inanimate landscape around him.

He came mooning along, and had nearly passed me, when, turning his head, he noticed me for the first time, and at once stopping and half turning round stood with his head raised, looking fixedly at me. I remained absolutely motionless, and the stag, after staring hard at me for some moments, turned and walked a few paces forwards. Then he swung round and stood looking at me again.

Two of the does now also stopped and stood looking either at me or more probably at the stag, whose whole attitude was full of suspicion. Then they moved on a little and turned and looked again, and continued so doing until they were some distance from me. They did not appear to have taken alarm, as

HEAD OF CARIBOU SHOT SEPT. 1, 1906.

they never ran, but just walked slowly away until they disappeared from view behind a ridge of stony ground.

They had hardly done so when I saw the horns of another caribou stag just showing above a swell in the ground in the opposite direction, and immediately my eyes caught sight of them I knew they were the horns of a big stag. The wind was perfectly right, blowing at the moment straight in my face.

I crept down into the hollow below me, and then ran rapidly towards the rising ground behind which I knew the big stag must be. I was within fifty yards of the foot of the rise, when I again saw his horns appearing over the top, and sat down to wait for him. But the top of his head had only just come into view when I felt an eddy of wind come from behind me.

Round went the great horns and immediately disappeared, and I knew that the stag had got my wind and at once turned and fled.

I ran forwards as hard as I could to the top of the rise but could see nothing of the stag, for he had very cunningly run down the hollow below the ridge, and then turned up hill again behind another swell in the ground. When I saw him once more he was quite two hundred yards away and galloping hard, and his horns then looked very large. I then, too, saw for the first time that he was followed by a very small caribou, a last year's calf, I should think. I had sat down and was just going to fire a running shot at the stag, with the two hundred yards' sight, when he stopped suddenly, and wheeling round stood looking back to try and get a sight of whatever it was, the smell of which had given him such a fright.

Now was my chance, and taking a steady shot I pulled the trigger.

I heard my bullet thud, and soon saw that the great stag was mine, for though he turned and galloped off again after being struck, he only ran slowly and heavily, and soon came to a stand, and I was able to get near and kill him with a second shot.

He was a fine big old caribou stag, standing between fifty-four and fifty-five inches in height at the shoulder, very heavily built, and in splendid condition, the fat over his loins being more than two inches thick.

His horns measured fifty-one inches in length, with an inside spread of forty-eight inches. They were, too, very massive, being nearly seven inches in circumference between the second and third tines. They were still in the velvet, but this was just ready to peel off, and I cleaned the horns on the spot, finding them fully formed, and sharp and hard at the points of all the tines. When I came up to the fallen stag, the calf, which somewhat curiously had been his companion, stood quietly looking at me from a distance of less than one hundred yards; and all the time I was engaged in cutting off the head, and disembowelling, and butchering the carcase of its late companion, it never went away, and often, when I looked up from my work, I found it had approached to within fifty yards of me. When I stood up and looked round it trotted off a short distance, coming up closer again when I was kneeling down beside the carcase

After I had skinned the neck and severed the head from the body I removed the headskin, and leaving the skull to be fetched by my men, made up as heavy a load of fat and meat as I could carry with the headskin and returned to camp.

Whilst I had been away, my men had brought in the hindquarters of the caribou doe shot the previous evening, so that we now had a plentiful supply of good meat and fat.

CHAPTER IX.

SPORT WITH BIG GAME IN THE MOUNTAINS OF THE MACMILLAN.

ON THE FOLLOWING morning I took my men to where I had killed the caribou the day before. We found a regular flock of ravens—there must have been at least thirty or forty of them—at the carcase.

As I had opened and disembowelled the carcase, and also cut the skin open all along the back, in order to get at the fat over the loins, the ravens had entered upon their feast under the most favourable conditions, and had not only entirely removed the great masses of fat round the kidneys but had burrowed in under the skin along the back, from which they had removed every particle of fat. They had also eaten almost all the soft meat of the loins and hindquarters.

In the mountainous regions of the Yukon ravens are excessively numerous, and in that wild northland these birds take the place of the vultures of the warm regions of the old world, spying out the carcase of any dead animal almost as soon as life has left it, and flocking in numbers to the feast.

As I prefer hunting by myself whenever I can do so, I sent

CARIBOU SHOT SEPT. 2, 1906.

both my men back to camp with the skull and horns of the caribou, and then went on by myself.

I had not walked more than a couple of miles, when I came in sight of a stag feeding on the top of a stony hill, which rose perhaps one hundred feet above the level of the surrounding country. On looking at him through my glasses I felt sure that he was a full-grown stag with fine large horns, and determined to try and get a shot at him.

To do so it was necessary, owing to the direction from which the wind was blowing, to make a long detour, and approach him from the further side of the hill. This I presently succeeded in doing, and on reaching the foot of the hill, I went down on my hands and knees, and crept slowly upwards, being careful not to make any noise by knocking the barrel of my rifle against a stone, for I expected to see the horns of the stag appearing above the brow of the hill at any moment. However, I presently crawled flat on my stomach right on to the highest part of it, and then at once saw a herd of ten caribou lying down on the open ground about three hundred yards away from the hill. This herd consisted of one big heavy stag with large antlers, and nine does and young animals, and as I could not see any other caribou stag anywhere in the surrounding country, I soon became convinced that the one which was now lying down with the herd was the same animal which I had first seen feeding alone on the top of the hill.

Whilst I had been working round to get at him from below the wind, he had left off feeding and rejoined the herd of which he was the leader.

To get any nearer to him without being seen seemed an absolute impossibility. There was a strong wind blowing, and a storm of sleet and snow was just coming on, so, putting up the three hundred yards' sight and taking a steady aim as I lay flat on the ground, I fired.

This shot missed the stag, but, as I afterwards found out, chipped a piece out of the side of one of his horns a few inches above the burr. He was lying at the time with his head turned round over his shoulder, so that my shot was in a good line but much too high.

Immediately I fired he stood up, as did two of the does, but the rest of the herd never moved.

The snow was now falling thick and fast, and was being driven into my face by the strong wind, but I was afraid that the stag would run off if I waited, so I fired again as quickly as I could, and by great good luck not only hit, but mortally wounded, him. I heard the bullet strike, and saw at once through the snow-laden air that the stag was done for, for he kept staggering about and soon lay down. I waited until the squall had blown over, and then walked down and killed him with a bullet through the lungs.

He proved to be a fine old stag with very massive horns, measuring forty-five inches in length along the main beam. A head well worth having. His horns were still covered with velvet, but were just ready to peel like those of the stag I had shot on the previous day. Later on, when I took his standing height at the shoulder, I found it to be fifty-four and a half inches, as near as possible.

Looking at my watch I found it was not yet one o'clock. I knew that if I were to cut open the carcase of the caribou and leave it, the ravens would eat all the fat before I could get back, so I resolved to make straight for our camp, and return at once with Coghlan and Thomas, so that we could carry the head, fat, and best parts of the meat away with us the same evening. I got back again with my men to where the dead caribou lay before four o'clock, and, after cutting him up, we again reached camp before dark.

On the following day, August 31st, Coghlan and Thomas

took the skulls and horns of the two caribou stags I had already shot, together with some fat and meat, down to our base camp on the river, returning in the evening with some additions to our small store of provisions. During the morning I was busy cleaning and preparing my two headskins.

In the afternoon I took a round over the ground to the left of where I had shot the first caribou, getting back to camp just as the night was setting in. I saw several caribou in little lots of two, and three, and four together, but they were all does and young animals.

On my return to the edge of the high ground overlooking the ravine in which our camp was situated, I saw our fire blazing cheerily in the gathering gloom, and I knew that my men had got back from the river. Not very long after that we all three sat down to a dinner of fat caribou steaks, with fresh-baked bread and tea, and what could a hungry hunter want better than that?

On September 1st I had a long day with Thomas, leaving Coghlan in camp. We first climbed to the top of the mountain to the right of our camp, and during the morning travelled over a great extent of what looked like splendid caribou ground, but we saw none of these animals with the exception of one doe accompanied by her fawn, until after midday.

We had just reached a point which commanded a fine view over a deep valley intersecting the high open mountains, when I noticed a black speck in the middle of a patch of last year's snow, on the shoulder of one of the mountains beyond the valley. Putting my glasses on to it, I saw at once that it was a caribou, and could just make out that it had got horns, and as it was alone I judged that it would probably be an old stag.

To get to him it was necessary to descend at least fifteen hundred feet to the bottom of the valley, and then climb as high on the other side. As we were approaching the low

CARIBOU SHOT SEPT. 2, 1906.

ground, which was covered with a growth of willow scrub, we disturbed a small herd of six caribou, two of them good-sized stags, but not, I think, very big ones. I was afraid that they might disturb the single stag, but they passed a good way below and out of sight of him, and presently I crawled on my hands and knees—having left Thomas behind—to the edge of the hollow filled with old snow.

The stag was no longer there, but I felt sure he had only just left it, and was still somewhere near. I first looked round very carefully, keeping my head low down, then gradually raised it higher and higher as my eyes swept over the uneven stony ground around me.

Suddenly I saw the tops of the stag's horns quite close to me, and splendidly palmated tops they were, too.

I knew he must be lying down within twenty yards of me, and in that open ground I knew, too, that however quickly he might spring to his feet and dash off he could not get away from me. So I rose to my feet holding my rifle at the ready.

The caribou was lying facing me, and so of course saw me, as soon as my head and the upper part of my body appeared above the contour of the ground. He immediately rose to his feet and stood staring at me. Poor brute! He was so near me that I could see his eyes quite plainly, and it seemed to me that they were full of a dreadful terror—the terror which unnerved Macbeth at the apparition of Banquo's ghost. His pain was short. One glance at his horns showed me they were very handsome, and in another moment I had sent a bullet through his heart. He just turned half-round, plunged madly forward for a few yards and rolled over amongst the stones, dead.

Did I feel sorry for what I had done, it may be asked? Well! no, I did not. Ten thousand years of superficial and unsatisfying civilization have not altered the fundamental nature of man, and the successful hunter of to-day becomes a primeval savage, remorseless, triumphant, full of a wild exultant joy, which none but those who have lived in the wilderness and depended on their success as hunters for their daily food, can ever know or comprehend.

The horns of this caribou were perfectly clear of velvet, which must, I should think, have been rubbed off a day or two before, as there was not a shred of it left on them, and they were dark red-brown in colour. They were very handsome and at the same time very interesting, differing entirely in type from all other specimens I have seen obtained in the Yukon territory.

As a rule the horns of the caribou from this district are very long and distinctly of the barren ground type, with the bez tine very much elongated and very slightly palmated. The horns of the animal I had just killed were only forty inches in length, but well palmated in all parts and with beautiful tops. They were, in fact, intermediate in form between the usually accepted barren ground and woodland types of horns, which shows how very difficult it is to classify the various races or species of caribou according to the shape of their horns.

Thomas had only just come up to where I was standing by the dead stag, when we saw another with a very fine pair of horns come up on to the top of a small hill about half-a-mile away. He stood there for a couple of minutes in full view and then went back again over the crest of the hill. I at once went after him but never saw him again.

I fancy that the six caribou which we had disturbed must have passed close to where this big stag was lying or feeding, and that, becoming aware from their manner that something had frightened them, he had gone up to the top of the hill to take a look round. He must have been suspicious of danger, as I went a good way beyond the little hill but could see nothing of him, though I came again on the herd of six.

It was quite dark before Thomas and I got back to camp

that evening, and we were quite ready for supper and bed. On the way home we saw two more caribou, one of which must have been a big stag, as his neck showed up very white. He was too far away to go after, however, as the light was already going.

The following morning I was just preparing to clean the headskin of the stag I had shot the previous day, when Thomas, who had gone to the creek to get water, called out that he could see a caribou just on the edge of the plateau above our camp, and that he thought he was a big one. When I went out with my glasses he was just standing on the sky-line, and I saw at once that his horns were very long.

I had no difficulty in getting up to and killing this stag. I found him lying down amongst some willow scrub just beyond the brow of the hill. His horns were quite clear of velvet and very long, measuring fifty-five inches over the curve, with a spread of forty-eight inches (inside measurement). Coghlan and Thomas took several photographs of him before cutting him up, and then brought his head and the best of the meat down to camp.

By the evening I had got both the headskins cleaned, and my men had cut all the meat off the skulls, which, on the following day, they took down to the river, returning the same evening. Whilst they were away I took a round over the mountains by myself.

About a mile beyond the little hill, near to which I had shot the second caribou on August 30th, I saw a lot of ravens fly up into the air, and judged that something must have disturbed them at the carcase. I hoped it might be a grizzly bear, so at once went to see.

Coming up under the wind and following a depression in the ground, I got within two hundred yards of where I had killed the caribou without giving any animal on the ground a chance of seeing me. Then raising my head I looked towards the remains of the caribou, and at once saw a black animal standing there, which I took to be a small black bear.

There were a lot of ravens sitting on the ground near it, and as many more hovering about in the air above. Some of these latter kept croaking loudly, and no doubt seen me. The black animal kept looking up at them, and was, I think, uneasy and suspicious.

As it was impossible to get any nearer to him than I was, I put up the two hundred yards' sight and tried to fire at him, but I had my rifle set at the safety, and before I could release it the black animal started off at a gallop. I was using an eight-millimetre Mannlicher rifle, with five shots in the magazine.

The black animal, which I never suspected to be anything but a small bear, did not run straight away from me, but in a half circle, skirting the base of a little hill, from the top of which I had shot the caribou. Still he always got further and further away.

I missed him with the first two shots, which both fell short. I then put up the three hundred yards' sight, and hit him in the hindquarters, my bullet doing him very little damage, as it only went through the flesh behind the bone of one of his thighs. It stopped him, however, for a few moments, during which he turned round and round several times, and was, I thought, going to fall, and so did not fire. But he soon recovered and went on again, though at a much slower pace.

I then fired my fourth shot, which I saw knock up some ground a long way short of him. I had one more cartridge left, but my moving mark was now, I verily believe, nearly four hundred yards away, and for some moments I held up my rifle, thinking it perfectly useless to fire again. Then I thought I might just as well empty my magazine, so, taking a very full foresight, and aiming well in front, I fired, and to my very great astonishment, the black creature immediately collapsed and rolled on the ground.

It was certainly a most remarkable shot, and I think that I might fire away a whole box of ammunition without ever again hitting so small a moving object at such a distance. Perhaps it was as well that neither of my men were with me, or I might have made a reputation which it would have been impossible to have lived up to.

When I came near the fallen animal I was. surprised and delighted to find that it was a black wolf—a fine large male.

In Alaska the large grey American timber wolves attain their greatest size, and a very handsome black variety appears to be not uncommon. These Alaskan wolves are said never to assemble together in packs, even in winter, but to hunt alone or two or three together. They are seldom seen in the daytime, and almost all the skins obtained are those of animals which have been poisoned, though some are trapped by the Indians. To have met with and shot in broad daylight a fine specimen of a black wolf was, therefore, a great piece of good luck.

I spent all the remainder of the day in skinning my prize and cleaning out the head and feet so that I could have it mounted whole.

On September 4th we returned to the cabin on the river, and on the following day took the canoe about fifteen miles further up stream to near the mouth of the Riddell River, named after the trapper of that name, who spent two or three winters in this district, and who, I believe, is the only white man who has ever penetrated so far up the south fork of the Macmillan River.

In the afternoon, as I was making my way along the bank about a mile ahead of the canoe, I saw a very large grey wolf on an open sandbar on the opposite side of the river. I got a very good shot at him at a distance of not more than one hundred and fifty yards, but unfortunately missed him. Whether I fired too high or too low I don't know, but anyway it was a very bad shot.

ON THE WAY DOWN THE MACMILLAN RIVER.

On September 6th we "packed" up into the mountains lying to the north of the river, and after a rough climb—very tiring with a pack on one's back—reached a point near the juncion of two streams in the neighbourhood of timber line which we thought would make a good site for a camp. After finding a level piece of ground we sat down on our packs for a rest.

From this point we commanded a good view up two valleys. My eyes had been wandering round for some minutes when they suddenly struck something about half-way up the hillside opposite, which looked to me like a moose lying down. I thought I could see the dark mass of his body surmounted by great white horns.

As far as my experience goes the horns of old moose bulls in the Yukon territory are always white—looking almost as if they were perished—when the velvet is first rubbed off them, and they remain white all September and during the early part of October. Whether they become brown like the horns of moose in Eastern Canada later on in the season I do not know.

Without taking my eyes off what I thought was a moose lying down, I took my glasses out of my pocket, and had just focussed them on to the spot, when Thomas, who did not know that I had seen anything, brought his axe down with a crash on a log of wood, and instantly I saw through my glasses a great bull moose rise from his bed and stand listening.

Of course I said at once to Thomas, "Don't chop, I can see a moose," but it was too late then. The animal had already taken alarm, and soon started at a trot up the hill. Hoping that he would soon stop I went after him, but never saw him again. I think he was a big bull, with very good, but not remarkably fine, horns.

Later in the afternoon, whilst my men were, engaged in getting our camp in order and collecting a store of dry wood,

I took a turn by myself, and came face to face with a very large wolf.

I was just approaching the open ridge of the hill behind our camp, but was still amongst a, scrubby growth of spruce, when I saw an animal coming down the same game path that I myself was following.

As the wind was right I stood perfectly still, and, raising my rifle to my shoulder, waited. I soon saw that the approaching animal was a wolf.

It came slowly down the game path, sometimes nosing about on the ground, and then walking forwards with its head up, but as I remained absolutely motionless it never appeared to notice me, though I was standing in full view, until it was within twenty yards of me. Then it halted, and stood gazing at me inquisitively, holding its head high and its ears pricked forwards.

Holding my sight on its chest, I now endeavoured to fire, but soon realized that my rifle—a single shot .375, by Holland—was set at "safe." To push the bolt forward I had to move my right hand very slightly. But this very slight movement at once caught the wolf's eye, and without waiting an instant he wheeled round, and was just going off at a gallop, when I fired and knocked him down. My bullet almost cut his tail off, and traversed the whole length of his body.

This was a very large dog wolf, as big, Coghlan said, as ever a wolf could grow, with jaws and teeth of tremendous power. It was brindled grey in colour, and in very good hair, though not of course in its thick winter's coat. I am sorry that I was not able to take a few measurements of this wolf before skinning it, as it seemed to me to be an animal of unusual size. But I had not my tape line with me.

We only remained in this camp three days, as we found nothing but old tracks of caribou and sheep on the mountains in the neighbourhood, which were very parched and dry compared with the range where I had been hunting caribou to the south of the river. I imagine that very little rain could have fallen in this district during the past summer, and that the feed having become poor and scanty most of the game had moved off in search of better grazing grounds.

We saw very little sign of moose either, amongst the willow scrub at the heads of the high valleys, and at this time, in this particularly warm season, I fancy that most of these animals were still low down in the thick forests.

I had, however, one piece of good luck at any rate. When out with Thomas on September 7th, we saw from the open shoulder of a mountain, a bull moose feeding near the head of a wooded valley some one thousand five hundred feet below us. I got down to, and killed him without much difficulty, and he proved to be a fine large animal with quite a pretty head, measuring fifty-three inches in spread, and having twenty-two points, eleven on each side.

This moose was in splendid condition, literally as fat as a stall-fed ox ; but we found that some time previously, probably in the early spring, he had received a bullet wound in the right shoulder, which had shattered the bone at the elbow joint all to pieces.

The wound, inflicted probably by the rifle of a trapper, had apparently given him but little inconvenience. There was no sign of inflammation round the wound, and no sloughing, the hole through the skin being filled with powdered bone. I cut the shoulder open and found several large pieces of detached bone loose amongst the muscles, and the solid ends of the bone were so far apart that I do not think they would ever have become united again.

It seems incredible that under these conditions the animal should have got into such splendid condition and grown so fine a head.

MOOSE SHOT IN THE MOUNTAINS, SEPT. 7, 1906.

On the morning of September 10th we returned to the river, where we at once lighted a big fire and dried all our belongings, as we were wet through more from the dripping trees and bushes than from the rain which had been falling steadily during the morning.

In the afternoon we loaded our canoe and started down stream for the cabin where we had left the caribou heads and some of our stores. This we reached in about two hours, though it had taken a whole day to get the canoe the same distance by poling and towing against the stream. We saw no game on our way down to the cabin; but it was raining hard all the time.

On the following day we again "packed" up to our old camp on the mountains to the south of the river. The whole landscape was shrouded in thick mist, but in the evening this all cleared off, the stars presently shone out, and the night became clear and frosty.

On September 12th I had a long day with Thomas on the tops of the mountains—which were now covered with new-fallen snow. A cold piercing wind was blowing over the high open ground. We soon saw a small herd of seven caribou (does and fawns with one young stag). When we first saw them they were feeding towards us, so thinking there might be a big stag behind we squatted down.

They came up quite near us before getting our wind, when they at once ran off.

After this we saw nothing more for a long time, but early in the afternoon, as I was walking a little in advance of Thomas, I suddenly saw first the horns and then the great white neck of a caribou stag appearing from behind the shoulder of a hill a few hundred yards in front of me.

Squatting down at once, I soon witnessed a sight which will long live in my memory.

One after another four magnificent old caribou stags

walked slowly one behind the other into full view on the open ground in front of us.

I had already shot four fine caribou, and I now only wanted two more—the head of one for myself, and the complete skin of another for our national collection at South Kensington.

All these four caribou were heavy old stags, and all of them carried such fine heads that it was a difficult matter to decide which were the best.

They presently got down into a hollow in the ground, and I was able to get quite near them. I might very easily have killed all four of them, as, after the two which I thought were the finest were lying dead, the other two did not run away, but stood still, evidently wondering what had happened to their companions.

These caribou had neither smelt nor seen me, and as they had probably never been fired at before, the report of my small bore rifle had conveyed no meaning to them. As soon as I showed myself, and walked towards them, however, they trotted off.

I must confess that it cost me an effort to allow them to do so, for they carried away two splendid pairs of antlers, certainly finer than those of the first three caribou I had shot, and since, as yet, there are no restrictions as regards the numbers of game that may be shot in the Yukon territory, I should have contravened no law but that of my own conscience had I added their heads to my collection of trophies.

I now examined the two slain stags. They were both magnificent specimens of the finest race of caribou on the North American continent. The horns of the one measured over fifty-seven inches in length, those of the other fifty-one inches, and they were both of them very big heavy animals in splendid condition.

I preserved the skin of the one with the longest pair of

horns very carefully, for mounting, and this splendid animal may now be seen in the mammalian gallery of the Natural History Museum, at South Kensington, side by side with a specimen of the Newfoundland race of caribou, which I brought home from that island in 1905. Both these specimens have been most excellently set up by Rowland Ward, the well-known taxidermist of Piccadilly, London.

Whilst Thomas and I were busy skinning the dead caribou, four more of these animals came feeding up the valley below us, and presently lay down on a knoll about four hundred yards away. I could see them very plainly with my glasses, and they were three big stags, two of them with very fine horns, and a smaller animal without any horns at all, which must have been a doe.

As I had shot as many caribou as I felt justified in killing, I did not allow myself to be tempted to take a nearer view of their heads, but just stuck to my work, and they presently got up and fed back again down the valley out of sight.

Leaving the skulls and horns to be fetched the next day, and burying a lot of fat meat under a bank of old snow, close to where the dead caribou were lying, Thomas and I "packed" the skins back to camp, which we reached long after dark.

On September 13th, Coghlan and Thomas went and brought in the heads, and some of the meat of the stags I had shot on the preceding day, whilst I remained in camp, cleaning and preserving the complete skin and hoofs of the one, and the headskin of the other.

On the following day my men carried the heads, together with some of our camp outfit, and a supply of meat, down to the river, as I now wanted to leave the caribou ground and look for moose in the forests on the lower slopes of the hills.

It was my intention, if I could shoot another good moose bull pretty quickly, to get back to Whitehorse as soon as

HEAD OF MOOSE SHOT ON SEPT. 15, 1906.

possible, and make a little trip after sheep from there, taking a couple of pack horses with me, so as to be able to move about.

In the Macmillan country, with no means of transport but the backs of three men, one cannot cover much ground after first "packing" up into the mountains, and as sheep rams band together in the summer and autumn, and keep to certain restricted areas, it is difficult to find them unless one can move camp continually and look over a lot of country.

On September 14th, whilst Coghlan and Thomas were carrying the caribou heads down to the river, I crossed the plateau to the left of our camp, making for the head of a deep thickly-timbered ravine, the bottom of which I intended to follow for some miles in the hope of coming across a moose.

I had just reached the further side of the level ground and was looking down into the ravine below me, when I saw a small flock of wild sheep on the hillside opposite. There were seventeen of them, all ewes and lambs. I could see them very plainly through my glasses, and watched them feeding about for more than an hour.

Although the heads and necks of all these sheep appeared to be snow-white, their backs and sides were of various shades of grey. Most of them were only slightly coloured, but two, and these both immature animals, were quite dark grey, and when in shadow looked quite black.

After descending to the bottom of the ravine I followed it down a long way, passing through many willow swamps where there was much old sign of moose, but I came across no fresh tracks of these animals, which I do not think had yet commenced to travel round as they would do later on in the season.

On the morning of September 15th we bade adieu to our camp on the caribou mountains, and making an early start, reached the cabin on the river before midday. We then loaded up our canoe at once, and in the afternoon made a start down the river.

We intended to camp for a few days near the forks of the Macmillan and hunt for moose in the neighbourhood of some lakes and willow swamps we had seen from the tops of the mountains in which we had lately been hunting caribou. As it turned out, however, I had the great good fortune to come on a fine moose bull, without doing any hunting.

Late in the afternoon, just before it was commencing to get dusk, we swept suddenly round a sharp bend :in the river, and came abreast of a little open glade running back between two belts of pine forest to a steep ridge. I was in the bow paddling, when I suddenly caught sight of what I knew were the tops of a moose's horns above the bank.

At the same instant the animal must have heard the canoe approaching, for he rose to his feet. Then he stood perfectly still right in the open ground and broadside on, with his head turned towards us. His great white antlers were spread out wide on each side of his head and looked immense!

Oh! could I but have photographed that mighty old bull as he stood there surveying us so proudly and so calmly. But there was no light for a photograph, and no time either, for the rapid current was carrying us fast down the river.

To change my paddle for my rifle was the work of a moment, and in another instant I fired, and—missed—yes, missed clean, a bull moose not thirty yards from me. It seems almost incredible, but it's true. I thought I had the sight on the centre of his shoulder when I pulled the trigger, but Coghlan and Thomas were trying to hold the canoe in the swift stream, and it was rocking badly and, anyhow, I missed.

I was using my single-shot rifle by Holland, and it took a second or two to get another cartridge into the breech. But the moose never moved a muscle until my second shot struck him fairly in the middle of the shoulder. Then he turned slowly round and walked towards the forest behind him. I fired again, as quickly as possible, and saw him fall to the ground.

Landing at once, Coghlan and I ran up to him. He was then lying flat on his side. I thought he was dead, and so put my rifle against a little bush and went up to examine his horns. When I was quite close to him he first raised his head, and then rose quickly to his feet.

Coghlan was then right in front of him, and the wounded moose at once made for him, I feel sure, with intent to do bodily harm, as he lowered his head and followed his enemy round, getting up pace at every step.

Coghlan and the moose were close to the bank of the river, when I got hold of my rifle and gave the latter another shot behind the shoulder. The bullet must have pierced his heart, I think, for he stopped in his stride, threw his nose in the air, and then fell over dead.

Coghlan was somewhat relieved, for, as he said, if the wounded moose had overtaken him before he got amongst the trees, it would have put him out of business.

This moose appeared to be a very old animal. The upper part of his body was very light in colour, he had not a particle of fat on him, and stank most offensively, although it was still only mid-September.

In a way his horns were magnificent, as they were perfectly symmetrical, with very wide palms, the measurement across which is now sixty-three and a half inches, and must have been over sixty-four when the animal that bore them was first shot.

Owing probably to the great age of this moose there were no points growing out from the tops of his antlers, and this takes away considerably from their beauty. A more remarkable characteristic of this head was that the small subsidiary palms or spikes, representing the brow tines of a red deer's head, were

HEAD OF CARIBOU SHOT ON SEPT. 12, 1906.
This specimen is now in the Natural
History Museum, London.

entirely wanting, though in all other moose heads I have ever seen I have never known them to be absent.

Although in the country through which the tributaries of the Yukon (the Hutalinqua, the Pelly, the Macmillan, the Stewart and the Klondyke) flow, moose may not grow, on an average, quite so large in size of body and antlers as their relatives in the Kenai Peninsula, they certainly approach that race—which has now been given sub-specific rank—in their proportions, and surpass in size and weight of body, and antlers, the moose of Central and Eastern Canada.

In 1904 I carefully measured the standing height of three bull moose-all of them old animals—shot on the north fork of the Macmillan River. These measurements were taken in a straight line between poles held, the one at the heel of the forefoot, the other at the extremity of the hair on the shoulder blade, and were six feet nine inches; six feet ten inches; and six feet eleven inches respectively. Measured in the same way, the hights of two full-grown bull moose, which I shot near Mattawa, Ontario, in 1900, were six feet one inch, and six feet two inches.

The length of the hair on the shoulders ought to be subtracted from all these measurements to give the actual height of body at the withers, but whether taken quite scientifically or not, all these measurements were made in the same way, and go to prove, I think, that the moose found in the East Yukon country, to the west of the Rocky Mountains, is a larger animal than the moose of Eastern Canada.

On the average, too, I think there can be no doubt that the moose of the Yukon country grow larger and heavier horns than their eastern relatives; in fact they seem to me to be intermediate between the eastern and far western races of this animal. Although in the East Yukon country a moose head with a spread of upwards of sixty inches is well above the average, such a head is much less exceptional in size than it would be in Eastern Canada.

In my own experience during two short trips to the upper Macmillan, I only saw six full grown moose bulls, and of these I shot five. The horns of the biggest had a spread of sixty-seven inches when first shot, and now measure sixty-six. Another had a spread of sixty-four inches (it now measures sixty-three and a half). The horns of the other three measured in spread fifty-eight and a half inches, fifty-three and a half inches, and forty-seven inches.

My largest pair of horns, when put on the scale at Selkirk, about a month after the animal to which they originally belonged was shot, weighed with the skull seventy-five pounds. The two horns in this specimen had not grown quite symmetrically. Had the right horn not been a little crumpled and bent inwards (probably from an accident whilst growing), but spread out in the same way as the horn on the left-hand side, these antlers would have had a spread of seventy-four inches. Moreover, this measurement would have been obtained, not between two long straggly points, growing out far beyond the width of the palms, but right across the middle of the palms themselves. The moose that carried this fine head was a very old animal, and I certainly think that had I met and shot him a year or two earlier than I did, I would have got a head measuring over seventy inches in spread.

In the mountain valleys of the East Yukon territory the feed for moose is very abundant, and these animals become excessively fat in the summer, and I see no reason to doubt that now and again antlers are produced in this district which would rival the largest and heaviest moose horns which have yet been obtained in the Kenai Peninsula of Alaska.

With the killing of the big bull moose on the evening of September 15th my second trip to the hunting grounds of the upper Macmillan River practically came to an end as far as shooting was concerned, for, with the exception of one young bull moose, which we saw feeding in a lagoon close to the river the day after we passed the cabin below Plateau Mountain, I met with no other game of any kind.

Going down stream at the rate of sixty or seventy miles a day, we reached Selkirk on the Yukon, without difficulty or incident of any kind, on the evening of September 20th, and four days later got back to Whitehorse by steamer.

Various reasons compelled me then to abandon my projected trip with pack horses after wild sheep in the country to the west of Whitehorse, and to return to England as quickly as possible.

On the whole I think I may consider that this short trip was a fairly successful one.

Its principal object was to obtain some good specimens of the magnificent caribou of the Yukon, and in this respect it more than fulfilled my expectations. In addition I had shot two very fine moose bulls and two large timber wolves, one a black one. I had failed once more to come across good specimens of either wild sheep or bears; but there are plenty of them in the wilder regions of the Yukon territory, and *"tout vient a qui sait attendre."*

CHAPTER X.

HINTS ON EQUIPMENT.

To ALL OLD travellers and hunters, any suggestions, as to armament and equipment for a hunting expedition, will be entirely superfluous. To younger men, however, who have not yet had much experience of big game shooting, and whose thoughts turn towards British North America as a field for the exercise of their energies, a few short notes on these subjects may possibly prove of some use.

RIFLES.

First as to rifles. It is difficult, perhaps impossible, to say which is the best weapon for American game, but any one of the wonderfully effective small-bore cordite rifles, now in general use by sportsmen all over the world, will be found good enough. Personally I have found a .303 and a .375 bore rifle, both by Holland, very effective weapons against moose and caribou, whilst several of my friends believe that the .256 Mannlicher is the best of all the small bore rifles.

Mr. P. B. Vanderbyl, as well as Mr. St. George Littledale, have shot all over the world with these wonderful little rifles, and both have killed with them very fine specimens of the gi-ant moose of Alaska; whilst my friend Mr. Charles Sheldon has been very successful in killing grizzly bears—the most for-midable of American animals—with one of the same weapons.

CARTRIDGES.

Having chosen a rifle—whether a Mannlicher, a Mauser, a .303 or a .375 bore—it is next necessary to procure car-tridges loaded with a good form of bullet, and this is a very important point.

What is required is a bullet that will expand when it strikes an animal but which will not break all to pieces im-mediately on impact.

The form of bullet which I long ago found to work very satisfactorily with a .303 rifle was the Government dum-dum, and since then I have never used any other kind. The principle of the dum-dum is to leave the lead at the top of a solid nickel-coated bullet slightly exposed. This causes the bullet to ex-pand but not to break into small pieces when passing through an animal.

Very few wounded animals will escape the hunter, or live long after having been struck with one of these bullets, and it is, therefore, a very deadly and at the same time humane form of projectile to use. Any ordinary military bullet, whether for the Mannlicher or the .303 rifle, can be quickly turned into a dum-dum, by rubbing down the nose on a rough file, until the lead is just exposed.

Altogether, I think that the modern hunter, armed with a small bore rifle and using dumdum bullets, is far bet-ter equipped for the pursuit of every kind of game than was his predecessor in the old days of black powder. If with such a weapon he should constantly fail to kill game, it will not be the fault of his rifle.

CAMP EQUIPMENT.

The next point to be considered is camp equipment. Wherever in North America pack horses can be used, or even Indian packers, there is no necessity to reduce the weight of one's outfit to the lowest possible point, and in such cases both tents and a profusion of bedding may be indulged in.

In those parts of the country, however, where there are no Indians, and where horses are not to be got, the sportsman himself and his one or two attendants will have to carry everything on their own backs, from the point where the canoe has been left on the river up into the mountains where he intends to hunt. In such cases weight is obviously everything.

To carry a tent big enough for three men, unless it is made of silk, is, under such circumstances, out of the question, but a piece of thin waterproof canvas sheeting, sixteen feet by twelve feet, which will only weigh twelve pounds, will be found to answer all the purposes of a tent.

In fact, in my own opinion, irrespective of the difficulties of transport, wherever in North America trees are to be found, a light waterproof canvas sheet is preferable for camping purposes to a tent. A cross pole is soon put up between two trees, and a lean-to made with a few saplings, over which the canvas sheet is stretched and brought well round at each end. This will keep out all rain and snow, and gives plenty of room for the hunter and his men, as well as for all stores, heads, skins, and so on.

In front of the lean-to a fire is lighted as large or as small as one likes, which makes the camp comfortable. A tent, besides being heavy to carry, cannot be warmed in cold weather except by a stove, which it is impossible to carry about in a country where there are no facilities for transport.

As for bedding, I have found that as soon as the temperature goes below zero, blankets are of very little use in proportion to their weight in keeping out the cold. What in Canada is called a "robe," that is, a covering made of the skin or skins of some animal, becomes absolutely necessary in cold weather. Wolf and lynx robes are considered to be the warmest. These robes are not always obtainable ready-made, but could be ordered beforehand at one of the big Canadian fur stores, such as Hope, Renfrew and Co., of Quebec. They must, however, be made large, at least eight feet by six feet, so that one can be wrapped completely round, and have both head and feet covered. These robes are, however, expensive, a good lynx robe costing at least fifteen pounds—now probably more, as the price of all fur has risen so much lately.

What I consider as good as anything in the way of bedding in a cold country is a Norwegian reindeer-skin sleeping bag. These sleeping bags could, I should think, be obtained through the Army and Navy stores. They cost in London about five pounds, and although they are somewhat bulky, they are very warm and light, not weighing more than sixteen pounds.

The next items to be considered in the way of camp outfit are cooking utensils. Of course there will be differences of opinion on this subject. Personally I always take with me the following articles:—Three aluminium cooking pots, fitting one inside the other, with one detachable handle, serving for all three. The largest of these pots is twelve inches high by eight inches in diameter. One large frying pan (twelve inches in diameter) with a stiff handle, a second smaller frying pan with a folding handle, three aluminium plates, cups, knives, forks and spoons. I always make tea in one of the aluminium pots, which saves carrying a kettle and tea-pot, and bake bread in the large frying pan, which necessitates a stiff handle.

Canvas bags of a light but well waterproofed material will be found very useful for carrying one's blankets and clothing on a canoe journey. Such bags, of any size required, may be obtained of Messrs. Lawn and Alder, 1 and 2, Brackley Street, London, E.C. This firm will also supply rücksacks of any size required, and made on the Tyrolese model.

When starting out on a long day's tramp in the mountains in search of game a small rücksack will be found very useful. In it can be carried some food, a little tea, an empty milk can to serve as a kettle, a small camera, and a sweater or cardigan jacket to put on if the weather turns cold or wet on the top of the mountains. A caribou headskin also can be carried back to camp packed in a rücksack more easily than in any other way.

CLOTHING.

In the way of clothing I have found in the early autumn in North-western Canada, where the climate is very changeable, a very thick light-brown cardigan jacket, made by the Jaeger Company, a very useful garment.

Sometimes it is very warm work climbing up a steep mountain in September. Then I put my cardigan jacket in the small rucksack which I always carry with me. When the top of the mountain is reached there is, perhaps a bitter wind blowing, and I then don my light, but warm jacket. I never wear a coat except in camp, nor a waterproof, preferring to get wet and dry my things over the fire.

For footgear in moose hunting before the snow falls, one requires something as noiseless as possible. Moccasins, which can be bought in the country, are very good, but it is not everyone who can walk long distances in them without getting his feet bruised, and personally I would recommend boots with thick red india-rubber soles. These are certainly liable to slip on a wet tree-root, but not more so, I think, than a saturated moccasin, and they are equally noiseless, and more comfortable for most Englishmen to wear.

Once the country in which one is hunting is covered with snow, one cannot do better than adopt the ordinary winter footwear of the western frontiersmen. This consists of what are known as German socks—which are thick felt stockings drawn over one's ordinary stockings, and reaching to the knee—and gum boots. These German socks and rubber boots can be bought in any frontier town in Canada, as well as clothing of every kind suitable to the climate of the country.

PROVISIONS.

The last point to be considered in the way of equipment for a hunting expedition in North America is the question of provisions. Here again the individual tastes of the hunter will have to govern his purchases. Personally, if I can get plenty of fat meat to eat and tea to drink, I find I can do very well without anything else but a little flour or biscuit. If I have the means of carrying it, however, I always take with me, in addition to bacon and flour, rice, dried apples, jam, butter, milk and sugar. From whatever frontier town one may start, however, on a hunting expedition in North America, it will always be found possible to lay in a stock of provisions of almost every sort and kind known to civilized man.

A tin or two of Symington's pea flour and a few pots of bovril (both of which must be taken from England) will often be found very useful. Two or three tablespoonfuls of pea flour mixed into a paste with cold water, will make most excellent soup if stirred into a pot of boiling water to which a sufficient quantity of bovril has first been added. When one is cold and wet and tired, a plate of this bovril pea soup, which can be made in a few minutes, will often be found most grateful and comforting.

As it is often a considerable time before it is possible to procure fresh meat, a light fishing rod and a small selection of flies ought always to be carried, as it will sometimes happen that many a good meal of trout or grayling may be caught before the game country is reached.

THE PRESERVATION OF HEAD-SKINS.

Should a large animal, like a moose or a caribou, be shot late in the afternoon in a country and at a time of year when you know that the temperature will fall below zero during the night, it is very necessary to get the head-skin off at once, before the carcase gets cold, even though the delay should prevent your reaching camp till late, or oblige you to remain where you are, sitting by a big fire all night.

Once a carcase freezes solid you will find it a most difficult matter to get the skin off the head.

In a cold country like Canada. it is not necessary to dress the head-skins of game with any kind of preservative, but all the meat should be carefully cut from round the lips, nostrils, eyes and ears, and the skins then thoroughly dried before being packed away. Should the weather be very wet, it will be necessary to dry such skins slowly and carefully by the heat of the fire.

If the nights are cold put the skins under your blankets and sleep on them to prevent them from freezing.

THE CARE OF THE RIFLE.

Just as one should take the greatest pains to preserve and bring home in good condition the head-skins of the game one has gone so far to find, so also should one take the greatest care of the rifle, to which in a considerable measure one owes the success of a trip.

I always carry a small funnel with me which fits into the breech of my rifle, and every evening on returning to camp, if I have fired but a single shot during the day, I pour two or three cupfuls of nearly boiling water through the barrel, and then rub it out dry with a cleaning rod.

In damp or rainy weather, vaseline will be found far better than any vegetable oil to keep the rust off a rifle, but in cold weather the springs and every part of the lock of one's rifle must be kept free of any sort of lubrication, as all kinds of oil will freeze, and may cause misfires through not allowing the mechanism to work freely.

INDEX.

CHECK OUT ALL THE
B&C CLASSIC BOOKS

—

AFRICAN GAME TRAILS

RANCH LIFE AND THE HUNTING TRAIL

By Theodore Roosevelt

—

A HUNTER'S WANDERINGS IN AFRICA

RECENT HUNTING TRIPS IN
NORTH AMERICA

By Frederick Courteney Selous

—

CAMP-FIRES IN THE CANADIAN ROCKIES

CAMP-FIRES IN DESERT AND LAVA

By William T. Hornaday

—

DRAGON LIZARDS OF KOMODO

By W. Douglas Burden

—

WILDERNESS OF THE UPPER YUKON

By Charles Sheldon

—

CPSIA information can be obtained
at www.ICGtesting.com
Printed in the USA
BVHW030522171121
621833BV00005B/49

9 781940 860448